Raised Bed Gardening

Beginner's Guide From A to Z to Growing Your Own Herbs, Vegetables and Fruit

Modern Green Lifestyle

Table of Contents

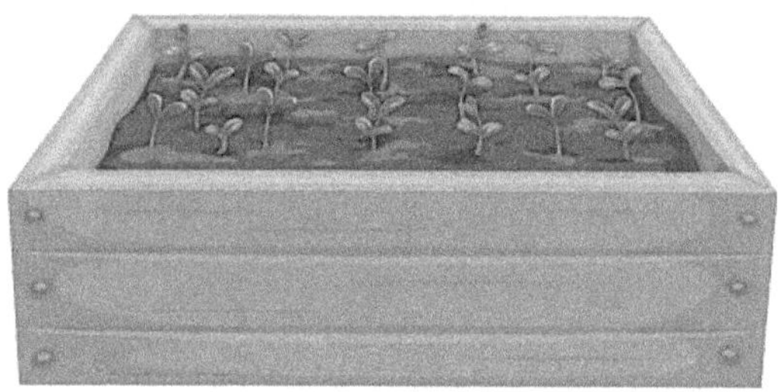

Introduction

A raised bed garden is a type of garden in which the soil level is elevated above the surrounding ground. Typically, this is accomplished by constructing a frame or box and filling it with soil around the garden area. Depending on the available space and the gardener's preferences, raised bed gardens can be constructed in various sizes and shapes.

The notion of raised bed gardening dates back to the Middle Ages, when the beds were generally enclosed by wattle fences. Almost 500 years later, the Parisian market gardeners of the 18th century used horse dung and compost to cultivate their plots in the pre-automobile era. Ultimately, they reached topsoil depths considerably in excess of one meter, and often two meters!
But, the raised bed concept as we know it now gained popularity in the early 1970s, when the construction consisted of digging a bed to a deep and fine tilth that was then built between roads. As a result of the rounded form of the bed, there was more surface area for plants to grow on, which, in conjunction with the increased planting density, enhanced production.

In addition to vegetables and herbs, raised bed gardens can also be used to cultivate flowers and other plants. Wood, stone, and even recycled materials such as old tires and shipping pallets can be used to construct them. The type of material utilized will be determined by the gardener's budget, preferences, and available resources.

Raised beds provide you control over the soil quality in which you cultivate your plants. A raised garden bed is just a mound of dirt or a bed of soil that is elevated above the surrounding terrain. The objective is to produce a large, deep growing area that stimulates the downward and outward growth of plant roots.

Benefits and Advantages of Using Raised Bed Gardens

- ➢ Raised bed gardens have greater drainage compared to traditional gardens, which is one of its key advantages. Due to the elevation of the soil, excess **water can drain more efficiently**, minimizing waterlogging and root rot. In addition, raised bed gardens tend to warm up more quickly in the spring, thereby prolonging the growth season.
- ➢ With a raised bed garden, **the soil can be modified to meet the unique requirements of the plants being produced**. Gardeners can use compost, fertilizer, or other amendments to create nutrient-rich soil that is perfect for producing healthy plants.
- ➢ Raised bed gardens can be erected at a height that is suitable for the gardener, making **gardening easier** for people with mobility challenges or impairments.
- ➢ **No soil compaction by foot traffic**. Due to the fact that raised beds are elevated from the ground, there is no foot pressure on the soil. This improves root development and is especially advantageous for soils prone to compaction. It also reduces the requirement for weeding because the soil is not disturbed during maintenance or harvesting. In addition, raised beds can enhance soil drainage and aeration, making

it easier for your plants to absorb oxygen and nutrients. Overall, the absence of soil compaction by human feet is a significant advantage of raised bed gardening.

➢ Because the soil in a raised bed garden is confined, **it is less likely to be affected by pests or illnesses** from the surrounding environment. In addition, raised beds can be protected from animals such as birds and rabbits by netting or other materials.

➢ **Fewer weeds.** Because the soil in raised beds is not in direct touch with the ground, it is less prone to weed seed dissemination. In addition, the soil in a raised bed is typically of a higher quality than the soil already present in a garden, which can prevent weed germination. Moreover, the soil can be modified with compost and fertilizer to decrease weed growth. Covering raised beds with fabric or plastic might further inhibit weed growth.

➢ **Massive advantage for gardeners with clay-rich soils.** Clay is notoriously difficult to control and drains poorly. The raised beds mitigate the drainage issue by increasing the soil's porosity and facilitating the drainage of excess water. This can have a significant impact on the health and growth of a plant. In places with clay soils that typically have drainage concerns, raised bed gardens are quite popular and liked by many.

➢ Raised bed gardens are **advantageous in locations with extremely sandy soil** because they retain water more effectively than typical in-ground gardens. The raised beds create a barrier between the soil and the air, which helps retain moisture and prevents excessive evaporation. In addition, the soil in raised beds heats up more quickly in the spring, allowing for early planting.

> **Optimize growth space in a restricted location**. The soil is lifted above the ground, allowing the gardener access to a greater volume of soil. This makes it easier to efficiently cultivate a variety of crops, herbs, and flowers. Also, the beds may be constructed to fit into compact areas, making them ideal for those with limited space.
> **The soil in raised garden beds is considerably warmer earlier** in the season than that in level garden beds. This enables you to begin planting sooner than usual, saving you time and increasing your yield. Moreover, the soil in a raised bed absorbs and retains heat during the day and night, making the soil even hotter. High heat accelerates plant growth and produces a larger, tastier harvest. For gardeners who wish to enjoy their harvest throughout the season, raised beds are ideal.
> **Warmer soil extends the growing season**. Since the soil is elevated above the ground, it takes longer for it to cool down at night, making warm-weather crops simpler to plant and allowing them to remain in the soil for a longer amount of time than if the soil were directly on the ground. This is particularly beneficial for those who wish to lengthen the growing season and optimize their produce.
> **Preserving soil from erosion**. Due to the garden's increased elevation, soil does not compact as quickly. Moreover, it remains in place and is not as easily transported by water runoff. Raised beds provide an additional layer of soil protection against strong winds and heavy precipitation. Due to the fact that fertile soil collects more readily at the bottom of raised bed gardens, the soil is not only protected from erosion but also from de-nutritification. This can lead to enhanced water retention, which helps keep soil in place and prevents erosion.

They have a longer growth season than traditional gardens due to their ability to retain heat, especially when constructed from materials such as stone or brick. As a result, they can warm up quicker in the spring, allowing plants to be planted earlier than in a conventional garden. The additional soil depth can provide plants with greater insulation, so delaying the onset of frost for longer durations. This can sometimes result in an extended harvest season, offering you more homegrown vegetables for a longer period of time during the growing season.

> **Excellent for assisting animals in the garden.** These gardens can give wildlife, birds, and pollinators with refuge, food, and a safe location to raise their young. Raised beds are frequently populated with plants native to the area's animals, providing a much-needed sanctuary for these creatures. They are also excellent for aeration, drainage, and the overall health of the soil, making the atmosphere more favourable to sustaining and nourishing the inhabitants.

> **Avoid polluted dirt**. With raised bed gardening, you may begin with soil that is devoid of herbicides, heavy metals, and other contaminants. This helps you to maintain the health, safety, and absence of potentially dangerous materials in the soil of your plants and vegetables.

> They are **ideal for novices** because they are simple to put up and require little upkeep. With raised beds, you have greater control over the soil's composition, drainage, and the possibility of soil-borne illnesses entering the garden. They also facilitate weeding and other tasks, such as harvesting, because you can reach everything without having to stoop. Additionally, raised beds allow you to efficiently organize and arrange your plants according to their height and size. This makes it easier to find what you need and makes everything

appear nice and organized. All of these advantages make gardening in raised beds an excellent option for beginning gardeners.

➢ **Your back is protected.** Raised bed gardens are ideal for individuals who do not wish to strain their backs using conventional gardening techniques. With a raised bed, you can work in your garden without bending over or digging into the dirt, so decreasing the strain on your back. Whether you have a pre-existing back ailment or simply wish to avoid damage, your back will appreciate not having to bend over constantly to tend to your garden!

➢ **They are temporary**. You may quickly alter or relocate your plan, allowing you to explore and develop your garden design as your preferences change. This implies that, unlike traditional in-ground gardens, you are not required to make a long-term commitment. In addition, setting up raised beds requires less effort because they do not require tilling or dirt backfill.

➢ **Aesthetics**: Various materials and shapes can be used to create aesthetically pleasing raised bed gardens. They are therefore an excellent addition to a backyard or outdoor living space. When constructing a raised bed garden, it is crucial to choose the most suitable location. The garden should be located in an area that receives plenty of sunlight and is relatively flat. To ensure that plants thrive, it is also essential to choose the proper soil mixture and to regularly water the garden.

Area Planning

Planning the area for a raised bed garden is essential for creating a successful and fruitful garden. Numerous factors must be considered, including location, space, layout, soil and drainage, and plant spacing. By taking the time to carefully plan, you can create a garden that will provide you with fresh produce throughout the season.

Consider **plant spacing**: While planning your raised bed garden, make sure to take into account the spacing needs of the plants you intend to cultivate. This will guarantee that each plant has sufficient area to develop and thrive. You may also try companion planting, which is growing several types of plants that mutually benefit one another, such as tomatoes and basil or beans and maize. It is essential to consider both the size and style of your raised bed garden while arranging the area for it. The size of your garden will depend on a variety of things, including the number of raised beds you want to utilize, the amount of area you have available, and how much you want to plant.

- Start by measuring the area where your garden will be located. This will give you an estimate of the amount of space you have available. Keep in mind that you'll need sufficient space for both the raised beds and any paths or walkways you intend to incorporate. You should also give sufficient space between beds to allow for comfortable walking and working.

- Secondly, think about the size of the raised beds you want to employ. There are many sizes of raised beds, ranging from little window boxes to enormous constructions with multiple levels. The size you pick will depend on a variety of criteria, such as the sorts of plants you wish to cultivate, the quantity of soil required, and your budget.

- Once the size of your raised beds has been chosen, you can begin to arrange the layout of your garden. Consider how you would want to position the elevated beds in respect to one another. You may choose to build a grid system with straight walkways or integrate curved walkways for a more natural appearance. Moreover, you can install trellises or other vertical supports for climbing plants.

It is essential, while arranging your arrangement, to give sufficient walking and working space between raised beds. A general rule is to provide at least 2 to 3 feet of distance between beds. This will provide sufficient space for comfortable movement and work.

- Consider the amount of sunshine the region receives while selecting the location of your raised bed garden. Vegetables and herbs require a minimum of 6 to 8 hours of sunshine every day to grow. Choose a site for your garden that receives sufficient sunshine and is not overshadowed by trees or other structures.

Determine the **location**: When choosing a location for your raised bed garden, consider factors such as **sunlight, access to water, proximity to your home**, and any other structures or landscaping in your yard. Ideally, you want a spot that receives at least 6-8 hours of sunlight per day and is level to prevent water runoff. You'll also want to make sure you can easily access a water source, either through a nearby hose or a rain barrel. Finally, consider how close the garden will be to your home, as you'll want it to be convenient to access when you're ready to plant, water, or harvest.

Sunlight is one of the most important factors to consider when planning the area for your raised bed garden. Plants need sunlight to grow and produce fruit, so it's essential to choose a spot in your yard that receives adequate sunlight. Here's a long and descriptive response on how to plan your raised bed garden area with respect to sunlight:

Determine the sunlight requirements of your plants: Different plants have different sunlight requirements, so it's important to choose a location for your raised bed garden that will meet the needs of the plants you plan to grow. For example, tomatoes and peppers require full sun, while leafy greens such as lettuce and spinach can tolerate some shade.

Choose a location with adequate sunlight: Once you know the sunlight requirements of your plants, choose a location in your yard that receives enough sunlight to meet those needs. Generally, you'll want to choose a spot that receives at least 6-8 hours of direct sunlight per day. Look for a spot that's not shaded by trees, buildings, or other structures during the peak growing season.

Consider the angle of the sun: In addition to the amount of sunlight, the angle of the sun is also important to consider. The sun's angle changes throughout the year, with a lower angle in the winter and a higher angle in the summer. To maximize sunlight in your raised bed garden, choose a location that receives full sun during the peak growing season (usually May through September in the northern hemisphere). You can also consider the angle of nearby structures, such as your house, which may cast shadows on your garden at certain times of day.

Plan for sun-loving and shade-tolerant plants: If you have limited space for your raised bed garden or a location with less-than-ideal sunlight, consider planting a mix of sun-loving and shade-tolerant plants. For example, you can plant taller plants that require full sun on the south side of your raised bed garden, while shorter plants that tolerate some shade can be planted on the north side.

Use shade cloth or other shading methods: In some cases, you may need to provide shade for your raised bed garden, especially during the hottest part of the day or during a heatwave. You can use shade cloth or other shading methods to protect your plants from excessive heat and sunburn.

When planning the area for your raised bed garden, one important factor to consider is the **proximity to your home**. Having your garden located near your home can provide numerous benefits, making it easier and more convenient to tend to your plants and harvest your crops.

Here are some reasons why you should consider the proximity to your home when planning your raised bed garden:

- Convenience: Having your garden located close to your home can make it more convenient to tend to your plants. This is especially true if you need to water your garden regularly or if you need to perform other maintenance tasks like weeding, pruning, or fertilizing. Being able to step outside your door and quickly tend to your garden can save you time and make it more likely that you'll keep up with the necessary tasks.

- Accessibility: Another advantage of having your garden close to your home is that it can be more accessible for people with mobility issues or disabilities. If you or someone in your household has difficulty walking or has other mobility challenges, having the garden located nearby can make it easier to access and work in.

- Pest control: When your garden is located near your home, it can be easier to monitor and control pests that may threaten your plants. You'll be able to keep a closer eye on your garden and notice any signs of pests or disease early on, which can help you take action to prevent them from spreading.

- Aesthetics: A garden located near your home can also add to the aesthetic appeal of your property. Raised bed gardens can be visually appealing, especially if you choose attractive planters and arrange them in an attractive layout. Having your garden close to your home can also allow you to enjoy the beauty and fragrance of your plants from inside your house.

- Accessibility to water: If you have a rain barrel or other water collection system, having your garden located near your home can make it easier to access water. You can simply use a watering can or hose to transport the water directly to your plants.

Access to water is an important consideration when planning the area for your raised bed garden. Here are some things to keep in mind:

- Choose a location near a water source: Ideally, you want to place your raised bed garden near a water source, such as an outdoor faucet or a rain barrel. This will make it easier to water your plants and help prevent them from drying out during hot weather. If your garden is not located near a water source, you may need to run a hose or install a rain barrel to collect rainwater.

- Consider the amount of water your plants will need: Different types of plants have different water needs, so it's important to consider the requirements of the plants you plan to grow. For example, tomatoes and cucumbers require more water than lettuce or herbs. Be sure to research the watering needs of your plants and adjust your watering schedule accordingly.

- Choose a watering method that works for you: There are several ways to water your raised bed garden, such as using a watering can, a hose, a sprinkler, or drip irrigation. Each method has its pros and cons, so choose one that works best for you and your garden. For example, drip irrigation is a great option for conserving water and delivering it directly to the roots of your plants.

- Consider adding a timer: If you have a busy schedule or are prone to forgetting to water your plants, consider adding a timer to your watering system. This will help ensure that your plants receive the appropriate amount of water on a consistent schedule.

- Monitor soil moisture levels: It's important to regularly monitor the moisture levels in your soil to ensure that your plants are not over or under-watered. A simple way to do this is to stick your finger into the soil to check for moisture. If the soil feels dry, it's time to water your plants.

Plan for soil and drainage: Before you begin building your raised beds, consider how you'll fill them with soil and ensure **proper drainage**. You'll want to choose a high-quality soil that's appropriate for the plants you plan to grow and ensure that the beds are deep enough to allow for good root growth. You'll also want to incorporate drainage holes or gravel at the bottom of the beds to prevent water from pooling and causing root rot.

Planning the area for a raised bed garden also involves considering **potential predators** that may pose a threat to your plants. Here are some things to keep in mind when planning to protect your raised bed garden from predators:

- Identify common garden pests: Before you can protect your raised bed garden from predators, it's important to know what you're up against. Common pests that can damage or destroy your plants include rabbits, deer, squirrels, birds, and insects like aphids and slugs. Each of these pests has different habits and behaviors, so it's important to research which pests are most common in your area and what measures you can take to protect your garden from them.

- Choose appropriate plants: Certain plants are less attractive to pests than others. For example, plants with strong scents or flavors like garlic, onions, and herbs can repel pests like rabbits and deer. Additionally, choosing plants that are native to your area can help deter pests, as they are more adapted to the local ecosystem and may have natural defenses against common predators.

- Build physical barriers: One of the most effective ways to protect your raised bed garden from predators is to build physical barriers. This can include installing fencing around the perimeter of your garden, or building a frame around each individual bed and covering it with bird netting or wire mesh. Be sure to bury the fencing or mesh at least 6 inches underground to prevent burrowing animals from accessing your garden.

- Use scare tactics: Scare tactics can be effective in deterring birds and other pests from your garden. Consider hanging reflective tape or CDs, or placing fake predators like owls or snakes near your garden to discourage birds and other animals from approaching.

- Implement natural pest control methods: There are several natural pest control methods you can use to protect your raised bed garden. For example, you can introduce beneficial insects like ladybugs or lacewings, which feed on common garden pests like aphids. You can also use companion planting, which involves planting certain types of plants together that benefit each other, such as pairing marigolds with tomatoes to deter pests. Additionally, you can make homemade pest repellents using ingredients like garlic, hot peppers, and soap.

- Monitor your garden regularly: Finally, it's important to regularly monitor your raised bed garden for signs of pest damage. Catching and addressing pest problems early can help prevent them from causing significant damage to your plants. Be sure to inspect your garden regularly and take action if you notice any signs of pest activity.

Size Considerations

When planning the area for a raised bed garden, one of the most important considerations is the size of the garden. Choosing the right size can help ensure that your plants have enough space to grow and thrive, while also making it easier to maintain and harvest your garden. Here are some long and descriptive considerations for sizing your raised bed garden:

Consider the available space: The first step in determining the size of your raised bed garden is to consider the amount of available space in your yard. This will help you determine how many raised beds you can comfortably fit in the area. Keep in mind that you'll need to leave enough space between beds to walk and work comfortably.

Think about your gardening goals: Another important factor to consider when sizing your raised bed garden is your gardening goals. Are you looking to grow a variety of vegetables, or do you want to focus on a few select crops? Do you want to have enough produce to feed your family or just enough for a few fresh meals each week? These factors can help you determine the size of your garden and the number of raised beds you need.

Consider your gardening experience: If you're new to gardening, it may be best to start with a smaller garden and expand as you gain experience. A smaller garden will be easier to maintain and can help you learn the basics of gardening without becoming overwhelmed. If you're an experienced gardener, you may be able to handle a larger garden with more raised beds.

Think about plant spacing: When determining the size of your raised bed garden, it's important to consider the spacing requirements of the plants you plan to grow. You'll need to leave enough space between each plant to ensure that they have enough room to grow and access sunlight, water, and nutrients. The amount of space you need will vary depending on the type of plant, so be sure to research the spacing requirements of each crop you plan to grow.

Consider the size of your raised beds: The size of your raised beds can also impact the overall size of your garden. If you're using pre-made raised beds, you'll need to consider their dimensions when determining the size of your garden. If you're building your own raised beds, you can customize the size to fit your available space and gardening goals.

Plan for future expansion: Finally, when sizing your raised bed garden, it's a good idea to plan for future expansion. You may find that you want to add more raised beds as your gardening skills improve, or as your family's produce needs increase. Leave enough space in your yard to accommodate future expansion, if possible.

Start Small!
Starting small is an important consideration when planning a raised bed garden. While it may be tempting to go big and create a large garden with multiple beds and pathways, it's important to remember that gardening requires time, effort, and resources. By starting small, you can test out your gardening skills and gain experience without overwhelming yourself.

Here are some reasons why starting small is important when planning the area for your raised bed garden:

- Manageable size: Starting with a small garden allows you to manage the area effectively. It's easier to keep track of the plants, soil quality, and water needs when you have a small area to focus on. This can help you avoid common gardening mistakes and ensure a successful harvest.

- Cost-effective: Building and maintaining a raised bed garden can be costly, especially if you're starting from scratch. By starting with a small garden, you can minimize the upfront costs and gradually expand your garden as you gain more experience and resources.

- Time commitment: Gardening requires time and effort, and it can be easy to underestimate how much work is involved. Starting with a small garden allows you to get a sense of the time commitment required and adjust your expectations accordingly. You can also build up your gardening skills gradually, without overwhelming yourself.

- Learning experience: Gardening is a continuous learning process, and it's important to give yourself the opportunity to learn from your mistakes. Starting with a small garden allows you to experiment with different planting strategies, soil types, and watering techniques without putting too much at risk. This can help you develop a better understanding of what works best for your garden and your specific needs.

Height
Here are some factors to consider:
Accessibility: The height of your raised beds will depend in part on your own physical abilities and needs. If you have mobility issues or prefer to avoid bending down to garden, you may want to opt for taller beds that are at least 24 inches high. If you don't mind kneeling or bending down to garden, you can choose shorter beds that are 12-18 inches high.

- Drainage: The height of your raised beds can also impact drainage. If your soil tends to be heavy or clay-like, you may want taller beds that allow for better drainage. On the other hand, if you have sandy soil that drains too quickly, you may want shorter beds that retain moisture.
- Soil Depth: The height of your raised beds will also depend on the depth of soil needed for the plants you plan to grow. Most vegetables require at least 6-12 inches of soil depth, while root crops like carrots and parsnips need at least 12-18 inches. If you plan to grow plants with deep roots or want to add amendments like compost or manure, you may need taller beds that allow for deeper soil.
- Cost and Materials: The size and height of your raised beds will also impact the cost and materials needed. Taller beds will require more soil, which can add to the cost, while shorter beds may require less soil but more building materials to create a wider base. Consider your budget and the availability of materials when deciding on the size and height of your raised beds.
- Aesthetics: Finally, the size and height of your raised beds can impact the overall look of your garden. Taller beds can create a more dramatic and structured look, while shorter beds can blend in more naturally with the surrounding landscape. Consider the overall aesthetic you want to achieve when deciding on the size and height of your raised beds.

Width
The width of your beds will affect how much space you have for planting, as well as how easily you can access your plants for watering, weeding, and harvesting.

Here are some things to consider when deciding on the width of your raised beds:

- Accessibility: One of the main benefits of raised bed gardening is that it allows you to garden without having to bend over or kneel on the ground. To make sure you can access your plants easily, you'll want to make your beds wide enough that you can comfortably reach the center from both sides. A width of 3-4 feet is generally recommended, but you can adjust this based on your own height and reach.
- Planting space: The width of your beds will also affect how many plants you can grow. A wider bed will provide more planting space, but may also require more soil and water. A narrower bed may limit your planting options, but can be a good choice if you have limited space or want to focus on a few select plants.
- Drainage: Another consideration when choosing the width of your beds is drainage. If your soil is heavy or prone to waterlogging, a narrower bed may be better as it will allow water to drain more quickly. If you have well-draining soil, a wider bed can be a good option as it will provide more space for plants to grow.
- Pathways: When planning the width of your beds, don't forget to consider the pathways between them. You'll want to leave enough space between beds for comfortable walking and working, but not so much that you sacrifice planting space. A pathway width of 18-24 inches is generally recommended.
- Aesthetics: Finally, consider the overall look and feel you want for your garden. A wider bed can provide a more substantial and impressive look, while a narrower bed can be more subtle and space-saving. Consider the other elements in your garden, such as walkways, trellises, and other

structures, and choose a bed width that complements the overall design.

Length

The size of your garden will depend on several factors, including the number of raised beds you want to use, the types of plants you plan to grow, and the available space in your yard. Here's a long and descriptive response on how to consider the size of your raised bed garden:

- Determine the number of raised beds: The number of raised beds you want to use will depend on the size of your yard and the amount of space you have available. Consider the types of plants you want to grow and how much space each one will require. You can use this information to determine the number of beds you'll need.

- Calculate the size of each raised bed: Once you know the number of raised beds you'll be using, you can calculate the size of each one. A standard size for a raised bed is 4 feet wide by 8 feet long, but you can adjust the size to fit your needs. Keep in mind that the beds should be narrow enough that you can reach the center from either side, usually no more than 4 feet wide.

- Consider the length of the beds: The length of your raised beds will depend on the available space in your yard and how you want to arrange them. Longer beds are great for growing crops that have a long root system, such as carrots, while shorter beds are better suited for crops that don't require as much space, like herbs.

- Plan for walkways: When planning the size of your raised bed garden, don't forget to factor in space for walkways. You'll need enough room to walk comfortably between each bed, so plan for a minimum of 18-24 inches between beds. You can also create a central path down the middle of your garden to make it easier to access all of your plants.

- Consider the overall size of your garden: When planning the size of your raised bed garden, consider the overall size of your yard and how much space you want to dedicate to gardening. If you have a large yard, you may want to create a larger garden with more raised beds, while a smaller yard may only have room for a few beds. Keep in mind that you can always expand your garden in the future if you have more space available.

Preparing

Turning a Lawn into Raised Bed Garden

Let's start with the most labor-intensive method of removing sod, which is cutting the turfgrass into small pieces and discarding them. This approach ensures that no grass or weed will grow through your new garden bed. However, it requires a lot of physical effort to remove all the pieces, including the roots. Additionally, this method may also remove some of the topsoil, which is essential for healthy plant growth. You can shake off as much soil as possible, but you may still need to amend the soil with organic matter like compost or fertilizer to ensure the soil in your garden bed is nutrient-rich.

An alternative method to remove sod is sheet composting or lasagna gardening. This method involves layering organic materials like cardboard, newspaper, and compost on top of the grass, which will gradually break down and turn into nutrient-rich soil. This approach takes longer than removing sod by hand, but it requires less physical effort and can improve the soil quality.

Another option is to use a sod cutter, which is a machine that can remove grass in large sections. This method is faster than removing sod by hand, but it can be costly to rent the equipment or hire a professional.

Regardless of the method you choose, it's important to remove all the grass and weeds from the area before building your raised garden bed. This will ensure that your plants have a healthy and fertile growing environment.

To convert a lawn into a raised bed garden, start by outlining the garden area using a garden hose, string, or stakes. Once you've outlined the area, water the planned garden area thoroughly to soften the soil. To remove the sod, use a half-moon edger or a sharp spade to cut the edges of the bed, and then cut the area into a series of narrow strips using the spade. Digging up the sod can be done with a variety of tools, but a sharp spade or shovel works just fine. Keep the spade at a low angle to get the roots while leaving most of the soil behind, and toss the sod into a container to compost or use it to patch other areas of your lawn.

One advantage of this method is that once it's done, you have a bed that's ready to plant without much planning. However, it does require a lot of physical work, which may not be suitable for those with back or joint issues. It's important to keep in mind that removing the sod can be labor-intensive, so it's a good idea to have someone help you with the task.

To make the process easier, you can use a sod cutter to remove the grass. A sod cutter is a machine that cuts through the grass and soil, making it easier to remove the sod in one piece. This method may be more efficient and less labor-intensive than using a spade or shovel.

Additionally, it's important to add soil amendments to the new raised bed to create a nutrient-rich growing medium. Mixing in compost, aged manure, and other organic matter can help improve the soil structure and fertility.

The solarization method is one means of transforming a grass into a raised bed garden. This procedure is especially effective if your existing lawn has a significant weed problem. To employ the solarization approach, cover the area of your planned garden with one or two layers of thick plastic, seal the edges of the plastic to keep the heat in, and leave it in place for six to twelve weeks, or until the sun's heat has baked and killed all living plants beneath the plastic. For weeds with exceptional persistence, such as bindweed, a solarization period of up to six months may be required.Once the grass is dead, remove the plastic and amend the soil before planting your raised bed garden. There is no need to remove the dead grass, as it will simply decompose and add nutrients to the garden soil. One advantage of this method is that it is a low physical effort approach. However, it does require patience since the process can take anywhere from six weeks to six months, depending on the amount of sun the area receives and the severity of weed infestations.

It's worth noting that solarization may not be effective in areas with dense shade or in climates with cooler temperatures. Additionally, this method may not be suitable if you have a limited timeframe for starting your garden. However, if you have the time and patience to wait, solarization can be an effective way to prepare your lawn for a raised bed garden, while avoiding the physical labor of manually removing the grass and weeds.

One approach to transforming a lawn into a raised bed garden is by smothering the grass. This involves covering the grass with a material that blocks air and light, causing the grass to die off naturally over several months. Common materials used for this method include old newspapers, cardboard, or chunks of carpeting. While this method requires little effort, it can take up to six months for the grass to fully decompose, making it important to plan ahead.

To start, determine the size and shape of your raised bed garden and gather the materials to smother the lawn. It's best to do this in late summer or fall so that the grass has time to die over the winter. Once the materials are laid over the grass, they will appear unattractive in the landscape, but this can be easily remedied by covering them with fall leaves or bark mulch. These materials can be pulled back when you're ready to plant in the spring.

One advantage of this method is that it requires very little work, and it effectively kills the grass, providing a blank canvas for your raised bed garden. Another benefit is that the dead grass will eventually decompose and become a source of nutrients for your plants. However, keep in mind that this method can take a while, and it's important to plan ahead to ensure that you have enough time to fully smother the grass before planting.

Lasagna gardening is a great way to convert a lawn into a raised bed garden, as it creates a nutrient-rich growing medium by layering organic materials over the garden area. This method is particularly useful if you want to avoid manually removing the grass and prefer a low-maintenance approach.

To begin, mark out the area where you want to create your garden beds, and then apply a thick layer of cardboard or newspaper over the grass. This layer will serve to smother the grass and prevent it from growing through the layers of organic materials. The next step is to layer a variety of organic materials on top of the cardboard. These materials should include compost that has been prepared, grass clippings, leaves, scraps of vegetables and fruit, decomposed manure, seaweed, shredded newspaper or junk mail, tea laeves, tea bags, pine needles, coffee grounds, and spent blooms and trimmings from the garden.

The layers of organic materials will slowly decompose over time, creating a nutrient-rich growing medium that is perfect for planting your vegetables, herbs, and fruits. However, it's important to note that this method requires patience as the bed needs to be built at least six months before planting. If food scraps are utilized, they may attract insects and animals that may be considered pests, and the decomposition of organic matter in the open air can occasionally generate odors that people find offensive.

The type of soil that you use in your raised beds is just as crucial as the materials that you use to create the beds themselves. It is important that the soil in your raised beds be nutrient-dense, have good drainage, and be devoid of any pollutants.

Here are some factors to consider when choosing soil for your raised beds:

Nutrients - The soil in your raised beds should be rich in nutrients to promote healthy plant growth. Look for soil that contains a mix of organic matter such as compost, aged manure, or worm castings, as well as minerals such as rock dust or bone meal.

Drainage - Raised beds should have good drainage to prevent water from pooling and causing root rot. Look for soil that is well-draining, and consider adding sand or perlite to improve drainage.

pH - The pH of your soil can have a big impact on plant growth. Most plants prefer a pH between 6.0 and 7.0. Consider testing your soil pH and adjusting it if necessary with amendments such as lime or sulfur.

Contaminants - The soil in your raised beds should be free of contaminants such as heavy metals or pesticides. If you are unsure about the quality of your soil, consider having it tested by a lab to identify any potential issues.

When filling your raised beds with soil, it is important to choose high-quality soil that is specifically formulated for use in raised beds. Avoid using garden soil or topsoil, which may not be well-draining or may contain contaminants.

In addition to choosing the right soil, it is important to maintain the health of your soil over time. Consider adding compost or other organic matter to your soil on a regular basis to maintain nutrient levels and improve soil structure. You may also want to consider rotating your crops each year to prevent nutrient depletion and reduce the risk of disease. By choosing the right soil and taking steps to maintain its health, you can ensure a productive and healthy garden in your raised beds.

Creating raised beds is an excellent way to turn a lawn into a garden, particularly if you have poor quality soil with issues like high clay content or acidity. To build a raised bed garden, you can use materials such as wood, stone, or concrete blocks to create a structure that is at least 8 inches in height around the perimeter of the garden area.

If the raised bed is at least 8 inches deep, you may not need to worry about smothering the grass below, as it will die on its own. However, if you prefer, you can lay down a few layers of newspaper before filling the bed. When the raised bed has been constructed, it should be filled with a combination consisting of high-quality garden soil that has been procured from a landscaping provider and organic additions such as compost or peat moss that has been properly mixed in.

One of the advantages of using raised beds is that you can create an ideal growing environment for your plants. You have control over the quality of soil, and you can add specific amendments to improve the soil's fertility, texture, and drainage. Another advantage is that raised beds provide better drainage and aeration, which can promote healthy root growth and prevent waterlogging.

However, there are some cons associated with creating raised beds, such as the cost of materials and garden soil amendments. Additionally, organic materials used in the raised bed may

decompose and produce an unpleasant odor if not properly managed. Another potential issue is that raised beds may attract animal pests such as rodents or slugs, which can damage plants.
In summary, building raised beds is a relatively easy and quick method to turn a lawn into a garden, and it offers several benefits such as creating an ideal growing environment, better drainage and aeration, and improved root growth. However, it is essential to consider the cost of materials and potential issues with organic material decomposition and animal pests.

Using herbicides to eradicate the existing grass is one strategy that may be utilized when converting a lawn into raised bed gardens. But, this approach is not appropriate for everyone, and there are a number of benefits and drawbacks to think about.
You will want a broad-spectrum vegetation killer that is effective against plants with blade-like leaves, such as grasses, in order to eradicate the grass. While many herbicides that are used to destroy plants also leave behind lingering residues in the soil, the most effective method is to employ a herbicide that is based on glyphosate, such as Roundup. Although new research shows that glyphosate, like other lawn pesticides, may have some cancer-causing qualities, it is considered to be a generally safe chemical since it is rendered inactive as soon as it comes into contact with certain soil enzymes.
Because the herbicide will destroy any plant material that it comes into contact with, you will need to carefully contain the spray to the area of grass that you wish to eradicate before applying it. Once the grass has died and gone brown and brittle, which might take up to a week, you will know that it is dead and be able to apply amendments to the area and then dig them in. There is no need to remove the dead grass; simply dig it in together with any amendments and more soil that you've added, and it will naturally

decay and contribute nutrients to the soil. There is no need to remove the dead grass.

While glyphosate herbicide is a quick and thorough way to kill grass, it's controversial and strongly criticized by organic gardeners. Glyphosate may be a safer chemical than some other herbicides, but it's still a chemical and must be used with great caution, if at all. Additionally, the dead grass can create a layer of thatch that may impede drainage and prevent proper root development in your raised bed garden. Therefore, it's important to add amendments such as compost or manure to help break down the thatch and improve soil quality.

If your space is currently weed-infested, you may need to take additional steps before starting a raised bed garden. One option is to use herbicides to kill the weeds, as described in the previous response. However, this may not be enough to completely eliminate the weed problem, especially if the weeds have deep roots or have already gone to seed.

Another option is to use a technique called "sheet mulching" or "lasagna gardening," which involves layering materials on top of the weeds to smother them and create a fertile growing environment for your raised bed. To do this, start by mowing the area as short as possible and then covering the entire area with cardboard or several layers of newspaper, making sure to overlap the edges to prevent weeds from poking through. Next, add layers of organic materials such as compost, manure, straw, leaves, and grass clippings, making sure to keep each layer moist. The organic materials will break down over time, smothering the weeds and creating a nutrient-rich soil for your raised bed.

It's important to note that this method can take several months to fully smother the weeds, so you may need to be patient before starting your raised bed. Additionally, you may need to supplement the soil in your raised bed with additional compost or other organic materials to ensure that it has enough nutrients for your plants to thrive. Finally, it's important to stay on top of weed control in your raised bed by regularly pulling any weeds that may sprout up.

If your space is currently covered in shrubs, you can still create a raised bed garden. However, the process will be different than if you were starting with a lawn.

First, you'll need to remove the shrubs. Depending on the size of the area and the number of shrubs, you may be able to do this manually with a shovel, pickaxe, or pruning shears. However, if the area is large or the shrubs are particularly dense or mature, you may need to rent equipment such as a backhoe or stump grinder.

Once the shrubs are removed, you'll need to prepare the soil. If the soil is compacted or poor quality, you'll want to amend it with compost, manure, or other organic matter to improve its fertility and structure. You may also need to level the area if the shrubs created uneven terrain.

Next, you'll need to construct your raised beds. Depending on the materials you choose, this could involve building frames out of wood, brick, or stone, or using prefabricated raised bed kits. Make sure to choose a location that gets adequate sunlight for the plants you want to grow.

Finally, you can fill your raised beds with soil and begin planting. You may want to choose plants that are well-suited to the growing conditions in your area and that complement each other in terms of height, color, and growth habit.

Overall, while starting with a space that is currently shrubbed may require more effort than starting with a lawn, it is still possible to create a beautiful and productive raised bed garden with a little bit of planning and hard work.

If your location is hardscape, such as a concrete patio or driveway, you can still create a raised bed garden with a little bit of creativity and effort.

The first step is to decide on the size and location of your raised beds. You can either create one large raised bed or several smaller ones. When choosing a location, consider factors such as sunlight, accessibility, and drainage.

Next, you'll need to create drainage holes in the hardscape to prevent water from pooling in your raised beds. This can be done by drilling holes in the concrete or using a hammer and chisel to create small indentations. Make sure to place the drainage holes in strategic locations to ensure adequate drainage.

After creating the drainage holes, you'll need to construct your raised beds. You can use materials such as wood, brick, or stone, or opt for prefabricated raised bed kits. Make sure the height of the raised bed is appropriate for the plants you want to grow.

Once your raised beds are constructed, you can fill them with soil and begin planting. Consider using a high-quality soil mix that is appropriate for the types of plants you want to grow. You may also want to add compost or other organic matter to improve soil fertility.

To care for your raised bed garden, make sure to water regularly and fertilize as needed. You may also want to consider installing drip irrigation to make watering more efficient.

The soil you use in your raised beds is just as important as the materials you use to contain them. The soil in your raised beds should be rich in nutrients, well-draining, and free of contaminants. Here are some factors to consider when choosing soil for your raised beds:

Nutrients - The soil in your raised beds should be rich in nutrients to promote healthy plant growth. Look for soil that contains a mix of organic matter such as compost, aged manure, or worm castings, as well as minerals such as rock dust or bone meal.

Drainage - Raised beds should have good drainage to prevent water from pooling and causing root rot. Look for soil that is well-draining, and consider adding sand or perlite to improve drainage.

pH - The pH of your soil can have a big impact on plant growth. Most plants prefer a pH between 6.0 and 7.0. Consider testing your soil pH and adjusting it if necessary with amendments such as lime or sulfur.

Contaminants - The soil in your raised beds should be free of contaminants such as heavy metals or pesticides. If you are unsure about the quality of your soil, consider having it tested by a lab to identify any potential issues.

When filling your raised beds with soil, it is important to choose high-quality soil that is specifically formulated for use in raised beds. Avoid using garden soil or topsoil, which may not be well-draining or may contain contaminants.

In addition to choosing the right soil, it is important to maintain the health of your soil over time. Consider adding compost or other organic matter to your soil on a regular basis to maintain nutrient levels and improve soil structure. You may also want to consider rotating your crops each year to prevent nutrient depletion and reduce the risk of disease. By choosing the right soil and taking steps to maintain its health, you can ensure a productive and healthy garden in your raised beds.

Building Structures

There are numerous types of raised garden beds, but the following are the most common:

- **Wooden raised beds** are among the most popular varieties of raised garden beds. They are typically made of rot-resistant wood such as cedar or redwood and can be fashioned in a variety of sizes and shapes. Wooden raised beds are relatively simple to construct and can be tailored to the gardener's specific needs.
- Stone or brick raised beds are an additional popular option. They are resilient and long-lasting, and they can add elegance to a garden. However, their construction can be more challenging and time-consuming than that of wooden raised beds.
- Container raised beds are raised beds constructed from containers such as plastic or clay pots, barrels, or other containers. They are an excellent choice for gardeners with limited space or those who wish to move their garden to follow the sun. Additionally, container raised beds can be used to cultivate plants that require specific soil types or to prevent the spread of invasive species.
- Additionally, there are raised garden beds made from recycled materials, such as old tires or pallets, and raised garden beds made from composite materials, such as recycled plastic. The type of raised garden bed that is optimal

for you will ultimately depend on your preferences, budget, and available space.

Materials

Raw wood can be a safe and effective material for containing your raised bed garden, but it is important to choose the right type of wood to ensure it is safe for your plants and the environment.

Some types of wood, such as treated lumber or wood that has been painted or stained, may contain chemicals that can leach into the soil and potentially harm your plants or leach into groundwater. These chemicals can include arsenic, creosote, and other toxic substances.

To ensure the safety of your raised bed garden, it is best to choose untreated, natural wood that is free of chemicals. Examples of safe wood types include cedar, redwood, and cypress, all of which are naturally resistant to rot, decay, and insect damage. Use wood that has been granted a certificate stating that it comes from a sustainable source, such as that granted by the Forest Stewardship Council (FSC) or the Sustainable Forestry Initiative. This is yet another choice for utilizing raw wood in your raised beds (SFI). These organizations make sure that the wood was gathered in a way that was not harmful to the environment and that it satisfies stringent requirements for environmental responsibility.

It is also important to note that while raw wood can be a safe option for containing your raised bed garden, it will eventually break down and need to be replaced. To extend the lifespan of your raised beds, you can line the inside with a barrier such as landscape fabric or plastic sheeting, which can help prevent soil from coming into direct contact with the wood.

One aspect to consider is whether or not wood **stains and paints are safe for use in contact with plants.**
Many wood stains and paints contain chemicals that can leach into the soil and potentially harm plants, animals, and humans. These chemicals can include heavy metals, solvents, and preservatives such as arsenic and creosote. Ingesting these chemicals can be toxic to plants, and can also pose health risks to humans who consume the plants.

However, there are wood stains and paints that are safer for use in contact with plants. Look for products that are labeled as "non-toxic" or "safe for use with food." These products are formulated with natural ingredients and are free of harmful chemicals.

Another option is to use untreated wood for your raised beds. While untreated wood will eventually break down over time, it is a safe and eco-friendly option for containing your plants. Cedar, redwood, and cypress are naturally resistant to rot and insect damage, making them excellent choices for raised bed construction.

If you do choose to use wood stains or paints, make sure to choose a product that is specifically labeled as safe for use in contact with plants. Apply the product according to the manufacturer's instructions and allow it to dry thoroughly before filling the raised bed with soil.

Treated wood is a popular choice for constructing raised bed gardens because it is affordable, readily available, and easy to work with. However, there is some controversy about the safety of using treated wood for growing edibles.

Treated wood is wood that has been chemically treated with preservatives to protect it from decay and insects. The most common types of treated wood for raised bed gardens are pressure-treated pine and cedar. Pressure-treated pine is treated with chemicals such as chromated copper arsenate (CCA), while cedar is often treated with copper naphthenate or another preservative.

While treated wood is effective at preventing decay and insect damage, the chemicals used in the treatment process can leach into the soil over time. This can potentially expose plants and humans to harmful chemicals, particularly if the raised beds are used to grow edibles.

The safety of using treated wood in raised bed gardens is a matter of some debate. The Environmental Protection Agency (EPA) has banned the use of CCA-treated wood for residential use, but other types of treated wood are still available. Some experts recommend using a barrier such as plastic or landscape fabric to prevent contact between the soil and the treated wood, while others suggest lining the beds with untreated wood or using alternative materials such as brick, stone, or concrete.

If you do choose to use treated wood in your raised bed garden, it is important to choose a type that is labeled as safe for use in vegetable gardens. Look for wood that is treated with newer, less toxic preservatives such as alkaline copper quaternary (ACQ) or micronized copper azole (MCA).

Ultimately, the decision of whether or not to use treated wood in your raised bed garden is up to you. While there is some risk of exposure to harmful chemicals, many gardeners have successfully used treated wood for years without any ill effects. If you are concerned about the safety of using treated wood, consider using an alternative material or taking steps to prevent contact between the soil and the wood.

Cinder blocks and concrete blocks are both commonly used materials for constructing raised beds. While they are similar in some ways, there are some important differences to consider when deciding which material to use.

Cinder blocks are made from a combination of cement and coal cinders, which are the ash and residue left over after coal is burned. They are generally less expensive than concrete blocks and can be found at most hardware stores. Cinder blocks are porous and may leach some minerals into the soil over time. This can be both beneficial and detrimental, depending on the type of plants you are growing. For example, if you are growing acid-loving plants like blueberries, the extra minerals may be beneficial. However, if you are growing plants that are sensitive to pH or mineral levels, such as certain herbs or vegetables, the minerals in the cinder blocks may cause problems. To mitigate this, you can line the inside of the cinder blocks with landscape fabric or plastic to prevent direct contact between the blocks and the soil.

Concrete blocks are made from cement, sand, and aggregate, and are more dense and durable than cinder blocks. They are also less porous and are less likely to leach minerals into the soil. Concrete blocks may be more expensive than cinder blocks and may be more difficult to find at hardware stores. However, they are a good choice if you want a long-lasting and low-maintenance raised bed.

When using either cinder blocks or concrete blocks for raised beds, it is important to consider the potential for leaching and to take steps to minimize any negative effects. This can include lining the inside of the blocks with landscape fabric or plastic, or using a sealant to prevent leaching. It is also important to make sure the blocks are level and stable, and to avoid using any blocks that are cracked or damaged.

Composite wood is a popular material for constructing raised garden beds due to its durability, affordability, and ease of use. Composite wood, also known as engineered wood or wood-plastic composite, is made from a mixture of wood fibers and plastic resin, which are combined and extruded into a variety of shapes and sizes.

One of the main advantages of composite wood is its resistance to rot, decay, and insect damage. This makes it a great choice for garden beds, as it can withstand exposure to moisture and soil without deteriorating over time. Additionally, composite wood does not need to be treated with chemical preservatives, which can be harmful to the environment and human health.

Another benefit of composite wood is its versatility. It can be easily cut, shaped, and assembled using standard woodworking tools, making it ideal for DIY gardeners who want to create custom-sized garden beds. Composite wood also comes in a variety of colors and finishes, allowing you to choose a style that complements your outdoor space.

Composite wood is also an eco-friendly option for garden beds. It is made from recycled materials, such as sawdust and plastic, and does not require the harvesting of old-growth trees. Additionally, composite wood can be recycled at the end of its useful life, reducing waste and minimizing its environmental impact.

While composite wood is generally safe for containing your garden beds, there are some things to keep in mind. Some types of composite wood may contain small amounts of volatile organic compounds (VOCs), which can be released into the air over time. To minimize exposure to VOCs, choose a low-emission composite wood product and allow it to off-gas for a few days before using it in your garden.

Railroad ties have traditionally been used as a material for constructing raised garden beds due to their durability, natural appearance, and low cost. However, there is growing concern over the safety of using railroad ties in gardening, particularly for edible crops.

Railroad ties are treated with creosote, a chemical preservative that helps to prevent rot and insect damage. Creosote contains several harmful chemicals, including polycyclic aromatic hydrocarbons (PAHs) and benzene, which can leach into the soil and potentially contaminate nearby plants and groundwater. Long-term exposure to PAHs and benzene has been linked to various health problems, including cancer, respiratory issues, and neurological damage.

Due to these concerns, many experts recommend against using railroad ties in raised garden beds. The EPA recommends avoiding using creosote-treated wood for any projects that may come into contact with food or drinking water. Instead, they recommend using alternative materials, such as untreated lumber, stone, or brick.

If you do decide to use railroad ties in your raised garden beds, there are steps you can take to minimize the risk of exposure to harmful chemicals. First, make sure to wear gloves and a mask when handling the ties, as well as when working in the garden. You can also line the inside of the beds with a barrier, such as plastic sheeting, to prevent soil from coming into direct contact with the ties.

Galvanized metal is a popular choice for raised bed garden construction because it is durable, affordable, and readily available. However, there are some concerns about the safety of using galvanized metal in contact with soil and plants.

Galvanization is the process of coating steel or iron with a layer of zinc to protect it from rust and corrosion. The zinc layer also makes the metal more attractive and gives it a shiny appearance. However, over time, the zinc can leach into the soil, potentially contaminating it with heavy metals.

Studies have shown that high levels of zinc in soil can be harmful to plants, reducing their growth and causing other health problems. In addition, the zinc can also be absorbed by the plants and eventually make its way into the food chain.

To minimize the risk of zinc leaching into the soil, it is recommended to use galvanized metal that has been coated with a non-toxic sealant. This can help prevent the zinc from coming into contact with the soil and plants.

Another option is to use a barrier between the metal and the soil, such as a plastic liner or geotextile fabric. This can help prevent direct contact between the metal and the soil, reducing the risk of contamination.

It's important to note that not all galvanized metal is created equal. Some manufacturers may use different coating processes or additives that can affect the safety of the metal. To ensure the safety of your raised bed garden, it's important to do your research and choose a reputable supplier.

Using tires as containers for raised beds is not recommended as they can leach harmful chemicals into the soil. Tires are made of synthetic rubber and various chemicals, including heavy metals, which can be released over time as the tires break down or are exposed to heat and sunlight. These chemicals can be harmful to both the plants and the people who consume them.

In particular, tires contain high levels of zinc, which can inhibit plant growth and lead to nutrient deficiencies. They also contain polycyclic aromatic hydrocarbons (PAHs), which are toxic compounds that can cause cancer and other health problems in humans and animals.

Furthermore, even if the tires are not actively leaching chemicals, they can still absorb heat, which can cause the soil to dry out more quickly and create an inhospitable environment for plant growth. Additionally, tires can be difficult to clean and sanitize, making them a potential breeding ground for pests and diseases.

Instead of using tires, it is recommended to use safe and non-toxic materials for raised bed containers. Some common materials include wood, brick, stone, concrete blocks, and metal. These materials are not only safe for plants and humans, but they also provide excellent drainage and can be easily customized to fit any space or aesthetic preference.

When choosing materials for raised bed containers, it is important to consider factors such as durability, cost, and ease of installation. For example, wood is a popular choice due to its affordability and ease of customization, but it may not be as durable as materials such as stone or metal. On the other hand, metal may be more expensive but provides excellent durability and longevity.

There are a variety of materials that can be used to create raised bed garden frames, including **premade kits.** The safety of these materials will depend on the specific type of material used, as well as how it is treated and maintained.

Some common materials used in premade raised bed kits include:

Wood - Wood is a popular choice for raised bed frames because it is readily available, relatively inexpensive, and easy to work with. However, not all types of wood are safe for use in raised beds. Avoid using treated wood, as it may contain chemicals that can leach into the soil and harm plants. Instead, choose untreated wood such as cedar, redwood, or pine.

Metal - Metal frames can be made from materials such as steel or aluminum. While these materials are generally safe for use in raised beds, it is important to choose metal that is not treated with chemicals that can be harmful to plants or humans. Some metals can also rust over time, which can be unsightly and may lead to structural issues.

Plastic - Plastic frames can be lightweight and durable, making them a good choice for raised beds. However, it is important to choose plastic that is safe for use in contact with soil and plants. Look for food-grade plastic or recycled plastic that is labeled as safe for use in garden applications.

Stone or concrete - Stone or concrete blocks can be stacked to create raised bed frames. These materials are sturdy and long-lasting, but they can be heavy and difficult to move or adjust. It is also important to choose stone or concrete that is not treated with harmful chemicals or additives.

When choosing a premade raised bed kit, make sure to read the product description carefully to ensure that the materials used are safe for use in contact with soil and plants. It is also a good idea to research the manufacturer and read customer reviews to get an idea of the quality and durability of the kit.

When it comes to creating raised beds, choosing the right materials for containing your soil is crucial. The materials you use should be safe, durable, and non-toxic to both your plants and the environment.

Here are some safe and popular options for containing your raised beds:

- Wood - Wood is a popular choice for constructing raised beds because it is readily available, easy to work with, and relatively inexpensive. However, it is important to choose untreated or naturally rot-resistant wood such as cedar, redwood, or cypress. Avoid using pressure-treated wood or wood that has been treated with creosote, as these chemicals can leach into your soil and harm your plants.

- Stone - Stone is a durable and long-lasting option for constructing raised beds. You can use a variety of types of stone, such as fieldstone, flagstone, or even stacked bricks. Keep in mind that stone can be more expensive and time-consuming to work with than other materials, and may require professional installation.

- Concrete blocks - Concrete blocks are another popular option for constructing raised beds. They are durable, long-lasting, and easy to work with. However, keep in mind that concrete can be more alkaline than other materials, so you may need to adjust your soil pH accordingly.
- Metal - Metal materials such as galvanized steel, aluminum, or corrugated iron can be used to construct raised beds. They are durable and long-lasting, and can be a good option for gardeners looking for a more modern or industrial aesthetic. However, keep in mind that some metals can rust over time, and may need to be treated or coated to prevent this.
- Plastic - Plastic materials such as PVC or HDPE can be used to construct raised beds. They are lightweight, inexpensive, and easy to work with. However, it is important to choose plastic materials that are food-safe and free of BPA and other harmful chemicals.

Raised Ground Beds

Raised ground beds are a popular gardening method that involves creating a garden bed that is elevated above the surrounding soil. There are many benefits to using raised ground beds for gardening, including improved soil quality, better drainage, and easier maintenance. Here are some key considerations to keep in mind when using raised ground beds in your garden:

Choosing the right location: When selecting a location for your raised ground bed, look for a spot that receives plenty of sunlight and has good drainage. Avoid areas that are prone to flooding or have poor soil quality.

Building the bed: Raised ground beds can be made from a variety of materials, including wood, stone, concrete blocks, or even recycled materials such as old pallets. When building your bed, make sure it is deep enough to accommodate the roots of your plants, and consider adding a layer of gravel or rocks at the bottom to improve drainage.

Filling the bed: Once your bed is built, it's time to fill it with soil. Consider using a high-quality soil mix that is rich in organic matter and nutrients, and avoid using soil from your yard, which may contain weeds, pests, or diseases.

Planting: Raised ground beds are a great option for a wide range of plants, from vegetables and herbs to flowers and shrubs. Consider the needs of your plants when selecting a location for your bed, and make sure to space them out properly to avoid overcrowding.

Maintenance: Raised ground beds require regular maintenance to ensure their continued health and productivity. This includes watering as needed, fertilizing periodically, and keeping an eye out for pests or diseases. It's also a good idea to rotate your crops each year to avoid depleting the soil of nutrients.

Supported Raised Beds

Simply put, a raised bed is a garden bed that is built above ground level and is supported by some form of structure, such as wooden or metal planks, cinder blocks, or bricks. The bed can be any shape or size, depending on the gardener's needs and available space, and can be used to grow a variety of plants, including vegetables, herbs, and flowers.

One of the most significant advantages of raised beds is that they provide excellent drainage. Because the soil is above ground level, water drains away more easily, preventing soil from becoming waterlogged and allowing plants to grow healthier roots. Additionally, the soil in raised beds tends to be looser and more aerated, which is better for root development and nutrient uptake.

Raised beds also allow gardeners to have more control over the quality of their soil. Gardeners can create their own soil mix, tailored to the needs of the plants they want to grow. For example, vegetable gardens might benefit from soil that is rich in organic matter, while a flower garden might require a more well-draining mix. By controlling the soil composition, gardeners can create an optimal growing environment for their plants.

Another benefit of raised beds is that they are easier to maintain than traditional gardens. The soil in raised beds is contained, which means that weeds are easier to control and gardeners don't have to worry as much about soil erosion. Additionally, because the beds are above ground level, they are easier to access and tend to, making it more comfortable for gardeners who may have mobility issues.

When it comes to building raised beds, there are several options for support structures. Wooden planks are a popular choice because they are readily available and relatively inexpensive. Cedar and redwood are popular choices for their durability and resistance to rot, but other types of wood can be used as well. Metal planks are another option and can be more durable than wood, but they can also be more expensive. Cinder blocks and bricks are a popular option for building raised beds as well, as they are long-lasting and readily available.

Containerized Raised Beds

Containerized raised beds are a type of raised bed garden that utilizes containers, rather than built-in structures, to create a contained growing space. Containerized raised beds can be made from a variety of materials, including plastic, metal, or even repurposed items such as old tires or wooden crates.

The benefits of containerized raised beds are similar to those of traditional raised beds, with the added advantage of being more portable and flexible. Containerized raised beds can be moved around to take advantage of changing sunlight or weather conditions, and they are ideal for small spaces or for gardeners who rent their homes and cannot make permanent changes to the landscape.

When selecting containers for a containerized raised bed, it is important to consider factors such as size, drainage, and material. Containers should be deep enough to allow plant roots to grow, and should have adequate drainage holes to prevent waterlogging. It is also important to choose containers made from non-toxic materials, particularly if growing edible plants.

Another consideration when using containerized raised beds is soil quality. Because containerized raised beds are self-contained, the soil in the containers must be of high quality to ensure optimal plant growth. Gardeners can create their own soil mix by combining compost, garden soil, and other organic matter, or they can purchase pre-made soil mixes specifically designed for container gardening.

Containerized raised beds can be used to grow a variety of plants, including vegetables, herbs, and flowers. When selecting plants for containerized raised beds, it is important to consider the size of the container and the size of the mature plant. Plants that grow too large for their container may become root-bound or stunted, while plants that are too small may not thrive in the larger growing space.

Before adding soil to a raised garden bed, it is necessary to prepare the bottom layer. The following are common materials for lining the bottom of a raised garden bed:

A layer of landscape fabric can be used to prevent weeds from growing through the soil. The fabric permits the passage of water and nutrients while preventing the growth of roots and weeds.

• Cardboard or Newspaper: At the bottom of the raised bed, place a layer of cardboard or several sheets of newspaper to prevent weed

growth. Over time, the cardboard or newspaper will eventually decompose, adding organic matter to the soil.
• Gravel or Rocks: To improve drainage, add a layer of gravel or small rocks to the bottom of the raised bed. This is especially useful if the soil in your area is dense or poorly drained.
• Compost or Manure: Add a layer of compost or manure to the bottom of the raised bed to enrich the soil with additional nutrients. This is especially useful if you live in an area with poor soil quality.

Noting that adding too much of one material to the bottom of the raised bed can reduce the amount of soil available for plant growth is essential. Aim to add no more than 1 to 2 inches of each material to the bed's bottom, and be sure to fill the remaining space with high-quality soil.

Planting

Planting a raised bed garden can be a fun and rewarding activity for anyone, regardless of their level of gardening experience. Raised bed gardens are particularly popular because they offer many advantages over traditional in-ground gardening. For example, they allow you to better control the soil quality and drainage, and they can be easier on your back and knees, as you don't have to bend over as much. Here are some tips to get you started on planting a raised bed garden:

- ➢ Choose a good location: The first step in planting a raised bed garden is to choose a good location for it. Look for an area that gets plenty of sunlight, as most vegetables need at least six hours of direct sunlight per day. The location should also be relatively level and free of weeds and grass, as you don't want those competing with your plants for nutrients.
- ➢ Build or buy a raised bed: Once you've chosen a location, you'll need to build or buy a raised bed. Raised beds can be made from a variety of materials, including wood, concrete blocks, or even straw bales. If you're building your own raised bed, make sure to choose a material that's durable and won't rot or break down too quickly.
- ➢ Fill the raised bed with soil: After you've built your raised bed, you'll need to fill it with soil. Use a good quality soil that's rich in nutrients and has good drainage. You can also mix in some compost or other organic matter to improve the

soil quality. It's important to fill the raised bed all the way to the top, as the soil will settle over time.

➢ Plan your garden: Before you start planting, it's a good idea to plan out your garden. Decide what vegetables you want to grow and how many plants you'll need. You'll also want to think about spacing and placement, as some plants will need more room than others. Make sure to take into account the height of the plants as well, as you don't want taller plants shading out shorter ones.

➢ Plant your garden: Once you've planned your garden, it's time to start planting. Make sure to follow the instructions on the seed packets or plant labels, as different plants will have different requirements for planting depth and spacing. You'll also want to water your plants regularly, especially when they're first getting established.

➢ Maintain your garden: Finally, it's important to maintain your garden throughout the growing season. This includes watering, fertilizing, and weeding as needed. You'll also want to keep an eye out for pests and diseases, and take steps to control them if necessary.

Choosing the right plants for your raised bed garden is essential for creating a thriving and productive garden. There are several factors to consider when selecting plants for your raised bed garden, including the growing conditions, space, and specific requirements of each plant.

One of the primary benefits of raised bed gardening is the ability to control the growing conditions, including the soil type and quality, drainage, and moisture levels. Different plants have different growing requirements, so it is important to select plants that are well-suited to the growing conditions of your raised bed garden. For example, some plants prefer well-draining soil, while others require more moisture.

Another factor to consider when selecting plants for your raised bed garden is the available space. Raised beds can be designed to accommodate a wide range of plants, but it is important to consider the mature size of each plant and ensure that there is enough space for each one to grow and thrive. Overcrowding plants can lead to poor growth, disease, and other problems.

In addition to space and growing conditions, it is important to consider the specific requirements of each plant. For example, some plants require more sunlight than others, while some are more tolerant of shade. Certain plants may also require specific nutrients or fertilizers to grow properly, and it is important to ensure that these requirements are met.

Choosing the right plants for your raised bed garden can also help to improve garden productivity and yield. Certain plants, such as legumes or brassicas, are known for their ability to improve soil health and fertility, while others, such as tomatoes or peppers, can produce high yields in a small space.

When choosing plants for your raised bed garden, there are several factors to consider to ensure the best possible growing conditions and a successful harvest. Here are some things to keep in mind:

Growing Conditions: Different plants have different requirements for soil type, drainage, and moisture levels. Consider the climate and environment of your region, as well as the location of your raised bed garden (e.g. full sun, partial shade), and choose plants that are well-suited to those growing conditions.

Space: Raised beds can be designed to accommodate a wide range of plants, but it is important to consider the mature size of each plant and ensure that there is enough space for each one to grow and thrive. Overcrowding plants can lead to poor growth, disease, and other problems.

Planting Time: Certain plants require specific planting times to grow properly. Some plants thrive in cooler weather, while others require warmer temperatures. It is important to research the planting times and growing seasons for each type of plant you plan to grow in your raised bed garden.

Companion Planting: Companion planting is the practice of planting different species of plants together that benefit each other by attracting beneficial insects, improving soil health, and repelling harmful pests. Consider incorporating companion planting techniques into your raised bed garden to promote healthy growth and a thriving ecosystem.

Pest and Disease Resistance: Some plants are more susceptible to pests and diseases than others. Consider choosing plants that are known for their resistance to common pests and diseases in your area to reduce the risk of plant damage or loss.

Harvest Time: The timing of the harvest can also affect plant selection. Some plants, such as lettuce or spinach, can be harvested continuously throughout the growing season, while others, such as tomatoes or peppers, have a shorter harvest period. Consider the timing of the harvest and plan accordingly.

There is a wide variety of plants that can be grown in a raised bed garden, depending on your climate, growing conditions, and personal preferences. Here are some plants that are well-suited for raised bed gardens:

Salad Greens: Lettuce, spinach, arugula, and other leafy greens are perfect for raised bed gardens. They grow quickly, require minimal space, and can be harvested continuously throughout the growing season.

Tomatoes: Tomatoes are a popular choice for raised bed gardens because they produce high yields in a small space. They require full sun and regular watering and can be grown using trellises or cages for support.

Herbs: Herbs like basil, parsley, thyme, and cilantro are easy to grow and add flavor to meals. They can be grown in small spaces and can even be grown indoors.

Peppers: Peppers, like tomatoes, produce high yields in a small space. They require full sun and regular watering and can be grown using cages or stakes for support.

Root Vegetables: Carrots, beets, radishes, and other root vegetables can be grown in raised beds with loose, well-draining soil. They require regular watering and can be harvested after the leaves have died back.

Beans and Peas: Legumes like beans and peas are excellent for raised bed gardens because they add nitrogen to the soil, improving soil health and fertility. They require trellises or other support structures and can be harvested throughout the growing season.

Cucumbers: Cucumbers require full sun and regular watering, but they produce high yields in a small space. They can be grown using trellises or cages for support.

Squash: Summer and winter squash can be grown in raised beds with ample space for the vines to spread out. They require full sun and regular watering and can be harvested throughout the growing season.

Berries: Strawberries, raspberries, and blueberries can be grown in raised beds with well-draining soil and ample space. They require regular watering and can produce high yields over several years.

Preparing your raised bed garden for planting is an important step in ensuring healthy and productive plant growth. Here are the steps you can take to prepare your raised bed garden for planting:

Clear any debris: Remove any rocks, sticks, or other debris from the bed. This will make it easier to work the soil and ensure that your plants have a clear space to grow.

Add organic matter: Add organic matter to the soil to improve its texture and fertility. This can include compost, aged manure, or other organic material. Mix the organic matter into the top few inches of soil using a garden fork or tiller.

Test the soil: Use a soil test kit to determine the pH level and nutrient content of your soil. This will help you determine if any amendments are needed before planting.

Amend the soil: Based on the results of your soil test, add any necessary amendments, such as lime or sulfur to adjust the pH level, or additional fertilizers to provide missing nutrients.

Level the soil: Use a rake or hoe to level the soil in the bed, removing any high spots and filling in any low spots.

Install a weed barrier: Cover the bottom of the bed with a layer of weed barrier fabric to prevent weeds from growing up through the soil. This will save you time and effort in weeding your garden later.

Create planting rows: Use a garden hoe or cultivator to create planting rows in the bed. Depending on the size of your plants, rows should be spaced between 12 and 24 inches apart.

Water the bed: Water the bed thoroughly before planting to ensure that the soil is moist and ready for planting.

Seeds and seedlings are both excellent options for starting your raised bed garden. Here is a long and descriptive response about seeds and seedlings:

Seeds:

Seeds are a popular choice for starting a raised bed garden because they are inexpensive and offer a wide variety of plant options. Here are some tips for using seeds in your raised bed garden:

Choose high-quality seeds: Look for seeds that are fresh, well-packaged, and labeled with the plant variety and planting instructions.

Start seeds indoors: Starting seeds indoors in a seed tray or small pots can give your plants a head start and help them grow stronger before they are transplanted into the raised bed. Be sure to follow the planting instructions on the seed packet and provide adequate light, warmth, and moisture for the seeds to germinate.

Direct sow seeds: Some plants, such as root vegetables, are best planted directly in the raised bed. Follow the planting instructions on the seed packet for proper planting depth and spacing.

Thin seedlings: Once the seedlings have emerged, thin them out to ensure proper spacing and adequate growth. Crowded seedlings can compete for nutrients and water, leading to stunted growth or disease.

Water seeds regularly: Seeds require consistent moisture to germinate and grow. Water them regularly, but be careful not to overwater, as this can cause the seeds to rot.

Seedlings:

Seedlings are young plants that have already sprouted and are ready to be transplanted into the raised bed. Here are some tips for using seedlings in your raised bed garden:

Purchase healthy seedlings: Look for seedlings that are healthy, with vibrant leaves and strong stems. Avoid seedlings with yellowing leaves or signs of disease.

Harden off seedlings: Before transplanting seedlings into the raised bed, acclimate them to outdoor conditions by gradually exposing them to sunlight, wind, and temperature changes over a period of several days.

Transplant seedlings carefully: Dig a hole in the raised bed that is slightly larger than the root ball of the seedling. Gently remove the seedling from its container and place it in the hole. Cover the roots with soil and firm the soil around the base of the seedling.

Water seedlings immediately: Water the seedlings immediately after transplanting to ensure that they have adequate moisture to begin growing in their new location.

Provide support for tall seedlings: Tall plants, such as tomatoes or peppers, may require support structures like stakes or cages to keep them upright and prevent them from bending or breaking.

Choosing the right seed or seedling for your raised bed garden is an important step in ensuring a healthy and productive garden. Here are some tips to help you select the right seed or seedling for your raised bed garden:

Consider the growing conditions: Before choosing a seed or seedling, consider the growing conditions in your raised bed garden. Factors such as sun exposure, soil type, and climate can all impact plant growth. Look for seeds or seedlings that are well-suited to the growing conditions in your raised bed garden.

Choose disease-resistant varieties: Certain plant varieties are more susceptible to disease than others. Look for seeds or seedlings that are resistant to common garden diseases in your area. This can help prevent plant loss and reduce the need for chemical treatments.

Research plant characteristics: Before choosing a seed or seedling, research the plant's characteristics, such as height, spread, and preferred growing conditions. This can help you choose plants that will grow well together and fit within the space in your raised bed garden.

Read customer reviews: Read customer reviews online or ask for recommendations from local nurseries or gardening groups. This can help you choose seeds or seedlings that have been successful for other gardeners in your area.

Choose reputable suppliers: Choose seeds or seedlings from reputable suppliers to ensure that you are getting high-quality, healthy plants. Look for suppliers that have a good reputation and offer a wide selection of plant varieties.

Consider planting times: Consider the planting times for different plant varieties when selecting seeds or seedlings. Some plants, such as cool-season vegetables, are best planted in the spring or fall, while others, such as warm-season vegetables, are best planted in the summer.

Method of growing

Prepare the soil: Before planting in your raised bed, it is important to prepare the soil. This involves removing any weeds or debris, loosening the soil, and adding organic matter like compost or aged manure to improve soil structure and fertility.

Mark planting areas: Once the soil is prepared, mark out the planting areas in your raised bed. This will depend on the plants you plan to grow and the spacing requirements for each plant. Consider using a grid system to ensure even spacing and make it easier to plan your planting.

Plant seeds or seedlings: Once you have marked your planting areas, it's time to plant your seeds or seedlings. Follow the instructions on the seed packet or container for proper planting depth and spacing. If planting seedlings, be sure to dig a hole slightly larger than the root ball and gently place the plant in the hole, covering the roots with soil and firming the soil around the base of the plant.

Water thoroughly: After planting, water your raised bed garden thoroughly to ensure that the soil is moist and the plants have adequate water to begin growing. Be careful not to overwater, as this can lead to soil erosion and waterlogging.

Mulch: Once your plants have begun to grow, add a layer of mulch to the soil surface. Mulch helps to retain moisture in the soil, suppress weeds, and regulate soil temperature. Organic mulches like straw, grass clippings, or leaves are excellent choices for a raised bed garden.

Provide support: Some plants, like tomatoes or beans, may require support structures like stakes, cages, or trellises to keep them upright and prevent them from bending or breaking. Plan ahead for support structures as you plant your garden.

Monitor plant growth: As your plants grow, monitor their progress and adjust as necessary. This may involve pruning, thinning, or staking plants as they grow. Be sure to remove any diseased or damaged plants to prevent the spread of disease.

Fertilize: Regular fertilization is important for maintaining healthy plant growth in a raised bed garden. Consider using a balanced fertilizer or organic options like compost or aged manure.

Water regularly: Regular watering is important for healthy plant growth. Water your raised bed garden regularly, being careful not to overwater or underwater. Consider using a drip irrigation system or soaker hose to ensure even watering and reduce water waste.

Here are some tips for maximizing plant growth in your raised bed garden:

Choose the right plants: Start by selecting plants that are well-suited to the growing conditions in your raised bed garden. Consider factors such as sunlight, soil type, and drainage when choosing plants. This will help ensure that your plants thrive and produce healthy yields.

Use high-quality soil: The soil in your raised bed garden should be a rich mix of compost and topsoil. Avoid using soil from your yard or garden, as it may contain pests or diseases that could harm your plants. Instead, purchase high-quality soil mixtures from a garden center or nursery.

Provide ample water: Raised bed gardens tend to dry out more quickly than traditional gardens, so it's important to water your plants regularly. Aim to keep the soil moist, but not waterlogged. Consider installing a drip irrigation system or using a watering can or hose with a gentle spray nozzle to water your plants.

Fertilize regularly: Plants in raised bed gardens often require more nutrients than those in traditional gardens, since the soil can become depleted more quickly. Consider using organic fertilizers, such as compost or fish emulsion, to provide your plants with the nutrients they need to grow.

Control pests and disease: Raised bed gardens are less prone to pests and disease than traditional gardens, but it's still important to keep an eye out for potential problems. Use organic pest control methods, such as handpicking pests or using insecticidal soap, to control pests. If you notice signs of disease, such as wilting or yellowing leaves, remove infected plants immediately to prevent the spread of disease.

Rotate your crops: To prevent soil depletion and reduce the risk of disease, consider rotating your crops from season to season. This means planting different types of plants in different areas of your raised bed garden each year. This can help keep the soil healthy and productive over the long term.

Provide support: Some plants, such as tomatoes or peas, require support to grow tall and strong. Consider adding trellises or stakes to your raised bed garden to provide support for your plants. This can help prevent damage to the plants and ensure that they grow to their full potential.

Best Herbs, Vegetables and Fruit to Grow in a Raised Bed - Plant Profiles

Artichokes

Artichokes are an edible plant native to the Mediterranean region, and they can be grown successfully in raised beds. They are a perennial plant that can produce edible flower buds for several years, making them a great investment for your garden. Here are some plant profiles for growing artichokes in raised beds:

Soil Requirements: Artichokes grow best in well-draining, fertile soil with a pH range of 6.0-7.0. Before planting, amend the soil with compost or aged manure to improve soil fertility and structure.

Sun Requirements: Artichokes need at least six hours of full sun per day to produce healthy and abundant flower buds.

Watering Requirements: Artichokes need regular watering, especially during dry spells. Water the plants deeply once or twice a week to keep the soil consistently moist.

Fertilizer Requirements: Artichokes are heavy feeders and benefit from regular fertilization throughout the growing season. Use a balanced, organic fertilizer high in nitrogen, phosphorus, and potassium.

Planting: Artichokes can be grown from seed or propagated from root cuttings. Plant artichokes in early spring, as soon as the soil can be worked. Space plants 3-4 feet apart to allow for their large size at maturity.

Maintenance: Artichokes require minimal maintenance beyond regular watering and fertilization. Remove any dead or damaged leaves as needed and stake plants to prevent them from falling over in high winds.

Harvesting: Artichokes are ready to harvest when the flower buds are large and plump. Cut the buds from the plant with a sharp knife, leaving a few inches of stem attached. Artichokes can be eaten cooked or raw, and they can also be preserved by canning or freezing.

Asparagus

Asparagus is a perennial vegetable that can be grown in raised bed gardens. Here is some information on how to grow and care for asparagus in a raised bed:

Soil: Asparagus prefers well-draining soil with a pH between 6.0 and 7.0. Raised beds are ideal for growing asparagus because they can provide the well-draining soil that asparagus needs to thrive. When preparing your raised bed for asparagus, amend the soil with organic matter, such as compost or well-rotted manure, to improve drainage and fertility.

Planting: Asparagus is typically grown from crowns, which are the root systems of mature asparagus plants. Plant the crowns in early spring, about 12 inches apart and 6 inches deep, with the buds facing up. Cover the crowns with soil and water them well. Asparagus can take a few years to establish, but once it does, it can produce for up to 20 years.

Watering: Asparagus needs regular watering, especially during the first year of growth. Water the plants deeply once a week, or more often if the weather is dry. Be sure to water at the base of the plants to avoid getting the foliage wet, which can lead to disease.

Fertilizing: Asparagus is a heavy feeder and requires regular fertilization. In the spring, top-dress the bed with compost or well-rotted manure. You can also fertilize with a balanced fertilizer, such as 10-10-10, according to package instructions. Avoid over-fertilizing, which can lead to excessive growth and weak plants.

Harvesting: Asparagus can be harvested when the spears are about 6-8 inches tall and as thick as your finger. Cut the spears at ground level using a sharp knife or pair of scissors. Do not pull the spears out of the ground, as this can damage the plant.

Maintenance: Asparagus can be susceptible to pests and disease, so it's important to monitor the plants regularly and take action as needed. Remove any dead or damaged foliage to prevent the spread of disease. You can also mulch around the plants to help retain moisture and suppress weeds.

Basil

Basil is an easy-to-grow herb that is a popular choice for raised bed gardens. Here's what you need to know about growing basil in your raised bed:

Planting: Basil can be grown from seeds or transplants. Plant your basil in well-drained soil with plenty of organic matter. Basil prefers full sun, but can also tolerate partial shade.

Watering: Basil likes to be kept moist but not waterlogged. Water your basil deeply once or twice a week, depending on weather conditions. Be sure to water the soil, not the leaves, to help prevent disease.

Fertilizing: Basil is a heavy feeder and benefits from regular fertilization. You can use a balanced fertilizer or a fertilizer high in nitrogen to promote leaf growth. Be sure to follow the instructions on the fertilizer package.

Pruning: Regular pruning will help your basil plants stay bushy and full. Pinch off the tips of the stems and any flowers that appear to encourage continued growth.

Harvesting: Basil can be harvested as soon as the leaves are large enough to use. Pinch off the leaves as needed, being sure to leave at least two sets of leaves on the plant to encourage continued growth.

Pests and diseases: Basil is susceptible to a number of pests and diseases, including aphids, whiteflies, and fungal diseases. Keep an eye out for any signs of damage or disease and take action as needed. You can use natural pest control methods, such as ladybugs or neem oil, or a chemical insecticide if necessary.

Companion planting: Basil is a good companion plant for tomatoes, peppers, and other herbs. It can also help repel pests such as mosquitoes and flies.

Beet

Beets are a nutritious and delicious root vegetable that are well-suited for growing in a raised bed garden. Here's what you need to know about growing beets in your raised bed:

Planting: Beets can be planted in early spring, as soon as the soil can be worked, or in late summer for a fall crop. Sow seeds about 1/2 inch deep and 1 inch apart, and thin the seedlings to about 3 inches apart once they've emerged.

Soil: Beets prefer well-draining soil that's rich in organic matter. Add compost or aged manure to your soil before planting to help improve its texture and fertility.

Watering: Beets need regular watering to keep their soil evenly moist. Water deeply once or twice a week, depending on weather conditions, to help promote healthy root growth.

Fertilizing: Beets don't require a lot of fertilizer, but you can give them a boost by side-dressing them with a balanced fertilizer once or twice during the growing season.

Harvesting: Beets can be harvested when they reach a diameter of about 1 inch. Use a garden fork or spade to gently lift the beets out of the soil, being careful not to damage the roots. Cut off the tops of the beets, leaving about an inch of stem, and store them in a cool, dark place.

Companion planting: Beets grow well with a variety of companion plants, including onions, garlic, and lettuce. Avoid planting them near pole beans or mustard plants, which can inhibit their growth.

Pests and diseases: Beets are relatively pest- and disease-resistant, but they can be affected by leaf miners, aphids, and fungal diseases. Keep an eye out for any signs of damage or disease, and take action as needed to protect your plants.

Bell Pepper

Bell peppers (Capsicum annuum) are a popular plant to grow in raised bed gardens, as they are relatively easy to care for and produce a bountiful harvest. Here are some plant profiles for bell peppers to help you get started:

Soil and Water Requirements: Bell peppers prefer well-draining soil with a pH between 6.0 and 6.8. They require regular watering, especially during hot, dry weather. Be sure not to over-water, however, as this can lead to root rot.

Sun Requirements: Bell peppers require full sun exposure to grow and produce a good harvest. Be sure to plant them in an area that receives at least 6-8 hours of direct sunlight per day.

Planting: Bell peppers can be planted in raised beds after the last frost date in your area. Space plants 18-24 inches apart and ensure that the soil is warm enough for optimal growth.

Fertilizing: Bell peppers benefit from regular fertilizing throughout the growing season. Use a balanced fertilizer with equal parts nitrogen, phosphorus, and potassium. Apply the fertilizer every 4-6 weeks.

Pests and Diseases: Bell peppers can be susceptible to a number of pests and diseases, including aphids, flea beetles, and bacterial spot.

Regularly inspect your plants for signs of damage and take appropriate action if needed.

Harvesting: Bell peppers are typically ready to harvest 60-90 days after planting, depending on the variety. They should be harvested when they are firm and glossy, and the color has reached its desired shade. Use pruning shears or a sharp knife to cut the peppers from the plant, taking care not to damage the stem or the plant itself.

Varieties: There are many varieties of bell peppers to choose from, including green, red, yellow, orange, and purple varieties. Some popular varieties include 'California Wonder,' 'Sweet Banana,' and 'Cubanelle.'Broccoli

Broccoli is a nutritious and delicious vegetable that can be grown in a raised bed garden. Here are some plant profile details to help you grow broccoli successfully:

Soil: Broccoli prefers a well-draining soil that's rich in organic matter. It also likes a slightly acidic soil with a pH between 6.0 and 7.0.

Sunlight: Broccoli needs full sun to thrive, which means at least six hours of direct sunlight per day.

Water: Broccoli needs regular watering, especially during hot and dry weather. Be sure to water deeply to encourage deep root growth, but avoid overwatering, which can lead to root rot.

Fertilizer: Broccoli is a heavy feeder and requires regular fertilization. Use a balanced fertilizer high in nitrogen, phosphorus, and potassium, or add compost to your soil to provide the necessary nutrients.

Planting: Broccoli can be grown from seeds or seedlings. Plant them in early spring or late summer, depending on your climate. Space plants about 18-24 inches apart to give them enough room to grow.

Care: To encourage strong growth and healthy plants, keep an eye out for pests and diseases and take action as needed. Regularly remove any yellow or damaged leaves to prevent the spread of disease, and apply organic insecticides to control pests such as aphids and cabbage worms.

Harvest: Broccoli is ready to harvest when the head is firm and tight, but before the flowers begin to bloom. Cut the head off at an angle with a sharp knife, and then continue to harvest the side shoots that will develop from the stem.

Cabbage

Cabbage is a cool-season vegetable that can be grown in a raised bed garden. Here's a plant profile to help you grow cabbage successfully:

Soil: Cabbage prefers well-drained soil that is rich in organic matter. A pH range of 6.0 to 6.8 is ideal for cabbage. Before planting, amend your soil with compost or well-rotted manure to add nutrients and improve drainage.

Sun and Water: Cabbage needs full sun to grow, but in hotter climates, it can benefit from some afternoon shade.

Cabbage requires consistent moisture, so be sure to water regularly, especially during dry spells.

Planting: Cabbage can be started from seed or seedlings. Start seeds indoors 6 to 8 weeks before the last frost date and transplant seedlings into your raised bed garden once the soil has warmed up. Space seedlings 12 to 18 inches apart, depending on the variety. Cabbage can also be direct-seeded into your garden in early spring.

Care: Cabbage requires consistent moisture to prevent splitting and ensure tender leaves. Water regularly, especially during hot, dry weather. Cabbage is also a heavy feeder, so be sure to fertilize regularly with a balanced fertilizer. Mulch around the base of the plants to help retain moisture and suppress weeds.

Harvesting: Cabbage is ready to harvest when the head feels firm to the touch and is fully formed. Cut the head from the stem with a sharp knife, leaving a few outer leaves intact to protect the head. If you harvest the head early, it will be smaller and more tender.

Pests and Diseases: Cabbage can be susceptible to a variety of pests and diseases, including aphids, cabbage loopers, and cabbage worms. Monitor your plants regularly for signs of damage and treat promptly if you detect any problems. Cabbage can also be affected by diseases such as clubroot and black rot, which can be prevented by practicing good garden hygiene and rotating crops.

Calendula

Calendula, also known as pot marigold, is a popular annual flower that is often grown for its bright, yellow or orange blooms. In addition to its aesthetic appeal, calendula also has medicinal properties and can be used in cooking. Here are some plant profile details for calendula in raised bed gardening:

Soil requirements: Calendula prefers well-draining soil with a pH range of 6.0-7.0. Raised beds with fertile soil that is amended with compost or other organic matter are ideal for growing calendula.

Sun requirements: Calendula needs full sun to thrive, which means at least 6-8 hours of direct sunlight per day.

Water requirements: Calendula requires regular watering to keep the soil moist but not waterlogged. It's important to avoid getting water on the flowers themselves, as this can cause them to rot.

Planting time: Calendula can be planted in early spring or late summer for a fall bloom. Seeds should be sown 1/4 inch deep and spaced 6-12 inches apart.

Care and maintenance: Calendula is a low-maintenance plant that requires minimal care. Deadheading spent blooms can encourage more flowering, and pinching back the stems can help to promote bushier growth.

Cantaloupe

Cantaloupe is a popular melon that is well-suited for growing in raised bed gardens. Here are some plant profile details to consider when growing cantaloupe:

Soil: Cantaloupe plants prefer well-draining soil with a pH between 6.0 and 6.5. Raised bed gardens can be filled with high-quality soil that has been amended with compost or other organic matter to provide the ideal growing conditions for cantaloupe.

Sunlight: Cantaloupe plants need plenty of sunlight to thrive. They should be planted in a location that receives at least 6-8 hours of direct sunlight each day.

Water: Cantaloupe plants require regular watering to stay hydrated, especially during hot, dry weather. In a raised bed garden, the soil tends to dry out faster than in a traditional garden, so it's important to water frequently to keep the soil moist but not waterlogged.

Spacing: Cantaloupe plants need plenty of space to grow and spread out. In a raised bed garden, plant cantaloupe seeds or seedlings at least 24 inches apart to allow enough room for each plant to develop.

Support: Cantaloupe plants can benefit from support to keep their vines off the ground and prevent them from becoming damaged or diseased. A trellis or other support system can help keep the plants healthy and productive.

Fertilizer: Cantaloupe plants benefit from regular fertilization to promote healthy growth and fruit production. A balanced fertilizer with equal amounts of nitrogen, phosphorus, and potassium can be applied every 2-3 weeks during the growing season.

Harvest: Cantaloupe fruits are ready to harvest when they're fully ripe and the stem begins to detach from the fruit. Be sure to pick the fruits promptly when they're ready to avoid overripening and spoiling.

Carrots

Carrots are a popular root vegetable that can be easily grown in a raised bed garden. Here's a plant profile for growing carrots in your raised bed:

Soil: Carrots prefer loose, well-draining soil that is free of rocks and other debris. Mix in plenty of compost or well-rotted manure to improve soil fertility and structure.

Planting: Carrots can be grown from seed directly in the raised bed. Plant the seeds ¼ inch deep and 1 inch apart in rows that are 12-18 inches apart. Once the seedlings emerge, thin them to 2-4 inches apart to allow room for the roots to grow.

Watering: Carrots need consistent moisture to grow properly. Water deeply once a week, or more often during dry spells. Avoid overhead watering, which can lead to disease.

Fertilizing: Carrots don't need a lot of fertilizer, but a light application of a balanced fertilizer can help them grow stronger and healthier.

Pest and Disease Control: Carrots are susceptible to pests such as carrot rust fly and diseases such as root rot. To prevent these problems, keep your garden clean and free of debris, and rotate your crops to prevent the buildup of pests and diseases.

Harvesting: Carrots are ready to harvest when the tops begin to turn yellow and the shoulders of the roots start to push out of the ground. Gently pull them out of the soil, taking care not to damage the roots.

Storage: Carrots can be stored in the refrigerator or in a cool, dry place for up to several weeks. Remove the tops before storing to prevent them from drawing moisture out of the roots.

Chamomile

Chamomile is a versatile herb that is often grown for its fragrant, daisy-like flowers, which are commonly used to make a soothing tea.

Chamomile is easy to grow in raised beds and can be planted as an annual or a perennial.

Here are some plant profile details for chamomile:

Scientific name: Matricaria chamomilla (also known as German chamomile or wild chamomile)

Plant type: Herbaceous annual or perennial

Mature size: Chamomile can reach up to 2 feet (60 cm) in height and 1 foot (30 cm) in width.

Sun exposure: Chamomile prefers full sun to partial shade.

Soil type: Chamomile grows well in well-draining, fertile soil with a pH of 5.6 to 7.5.

Soil moisture: Chamomile prefers moist soil but can tolerate drought conditions.

Bloom time: Chamomile typically blooms in the late spring or early summer and may continue to bloom sporadically throughout the growing season.

Flower color: Chamomile flowers are white with yellow centers and have a pleasant, apple-like fragrance.

Chives

Chives are a popular herb that can be easily grown in a raised bed garden. Here are some plant profile details:

Plant Description: Chives (Allium schoenoprasum) are a member of the onion family and have a grass-like appearance with long, slender leaves that can grow up to 20 inches tall. The leaves are hollow and have a mild onion flavor that is commonly used in soups, stews, and salads.

Planting: Chives can be planted in the spring or fall, and prefer well-drained soil with full sun exposure. They can be grown from seed or purchased as seedlings, and should be planted in small groups about 6 inches apart. When planting, be sure to keep the soil moist but not waterlogged.

Care: Chives are easy to care for and require minimal maintenance. They should be watered regularly to keep the soil moist, but not overwatered. Fertilizing with a balanced fertilizer once a month can help promote growth. Chives can also be cut back to encourage new growth and prevent the plant from flowering.

Harvesting: Chives can be harvested once the leaves have reached about 6 inches in length. To harvest, use a sharp pair of scissors to cut the leaves close to the base of the plant. It's important to leave some leaves on the plant so it can continue to grow and produce.

Pests and Diseases: Chives are generally resistant to pests and diseases. However, they can be susceptible to onion maggots, thrips, and leafminers. Regular monitoring and prompt treatment with insecticides or organic pest control methods can help prevent damage to your plants.

Culinary Uses: Chives are commonly used in a variety of dishes, including soups, stews, omelets, and salads. They can also be used to make a flavorful chive butter or added to dips and spreads.

Cilantro

Cilantro, also known as coriander, is a popular herb that is commonly used in Mexican, Thai, and Indian cuisine. It's easy to grow in a raised bed garden and can provide a bountiful harvest with the right care and attention. Here are some plant profile details for cilantro:

Soil requirements: Cilantro prefers well-draining soil that is rich in organic matter. A soil pH between 6.0 and 7.0 is ideal.

Sun requirements: Cilantro prefers partial shade to full sun, but in hot climates, it may benefit from some shade during the hottest part of the day.

Water requirements: Cilantro prefers consistently moist soil. Water deeply once a week or as needed to keep the soil moist, but not waterlogged.

Fertilizer requirements: Cilantro doesn't require much fertilizer, but adding a balanced fertilizer once a month can help encourage healthy growth.

Harvesting: Cilantro leaves can be harvested as soon as the plant reaches 6 inches in height. Simply snip off the outermost leaves with a pair of scissors. Be sure to leave at least 1 inch of growth at the base of the plant to encourage continued growth.

Pests and diseases: Cilantro is relatively pest-resistant, but it can be prone to fungal diseases in humid climates. Be sure to provide good air circulation around the plants to help prevent disease.

Companion plants: Cilantro grows well with other herbs, such as parsley and basil, as well as with vegetables like tomatoes and peppers.

Corn

Corn is a warm-season crop that can thrive in a raised bed garden if provided with the right growing conditions. Here's what you need to know about planting and growing corn in your raised bed garden:

Planting: Corn should be planted in soil that has reached a temperature of at least 60 degrees Fahrenheit, which typically occurs in late spring or early summer. Sow seeds directly into the soil, spacing them 8-12 inches apart and 1-2 inches deep.

Soil: Corn prefers well-draining soil that is rich in organic matter. Amend your soil with compost or well-rotted manure before planting to provide the nutrients that corn needs to grow.

Watering: Corn needs regular, deep watering to thrive. Aim to give your corn plants at least 1 inch of water per week, either through rainfall or supplemental irrigation.

Fertilizing: Corn is a heavy feeder and will benefit from regular applications of fertilizer throughout the growing season. Use a balanced fertilizer with a ratio of 10-10-10, applying it at a rate of 1 pound per 100 square feet of garden bed.

Support: Corn plants can grow quite tall, reaching heights of 6-8 feet in some cases. To support your plants, stake them or use a trellis system to prevent them from falling over or breaking in strong winds.

Harvesting: Corn is typically ready to harvest 70-100 days after planting, depending on the variety. Look for ears that are firm and well-filled with kernels. To harvest, grasp the ear firmly and twist it off the stalk.

Cucumbers

Cucumbers are a popular vegetable to grow in raised bed gardens because they are easy to grow, produce a high yield, and are versatile in the kitchen. Here are some plant profile details for cucumbers:

Growing conditions: Cucumbers thrive in warm, sunny locations with well-drained soil. They prefer soil that is slightly acidic with a pH between 6.0 and 7.0. Cucumbers also need consistent moisture, so it's important to water them regularly.

Planting: Cucumber seeds can be started indoors about four weeks before the last frost date, or they can be directly sown into the garden once the soil has warmed up in the spring. When planting, be sure to provide adequate spacing between plants to allow for good air circulation and prevent overcrowding.

Care: Cucumbers are heavy feeders and require regular fertilization. You can apply a balanced fertilizer once a month during the growing season to keep them healthy and productive. Additionally, it's important to keep the soil consistently moist, especially during hot and dry weather.

Harvesting: Cucumbers are ready to harvest when they are about six to eight inches long and have a bright green color. Be sure to check your plants frequently and pick the cucumbers as soon as they are ripe to encourage continued production.

Pest and disease management: Cucumbers are susceptible to several pests and diseases, including cucumber beetles, powdery mildew, and downy mildew. To prevent these issues, practice good garden hygiene, such as removing plant debris and avoiding overhead watering. You can also use natural pest control methods, such as companion planting and insecticidal soap.

Culinary uses: Cucumbers are a versatile vegetable that can be used in a variety of dishes, from salads to sandwiches. They can be eaten raw or cooked and are often pickled for a tangy, crunchy snack.

Cumin

Cumin (Cuminum cyminum) is a plant that belongs to the parsley family, and it is commonly grown for its seeds, which are used as a spice in many cuisines around the world. Here are some plant profiles for growing cumin in a raised bed garden:

Soil: Cumin prefers well-draining soil with a pH range of 6.0 to 7.5. Raised beds filled with a mix of loamy soil, sand, and compost can provide the ideal growing conditions for cumin.

Sunlight: Cumin requires full sun exposure, at least six hours of direct sunlight daily.

Watering: Cumin needs moderate watering, but it should not be over-watered as this can cause root rot. Soil should be moist but not waterlogged. Watering every 4-5 days is usually sufficient, but be mindful of the weather conditions.

Temperature: Cumin is a warm-season crop and requires a temperature range of 20-30°C. Sow seeds once the temperature has reached at least 15°C in early summer.

Planting: Cumin can be directly sowed into raised beds or started indoors before transplanting. Sow seeds at a depth of 1/4 inch and space them 4-6 inches apart. Germination typically occurs within 7-14 days.

Maintenance: Weeding is important to prevent competition for nutrients, and the soil should be kept moist. Cumin does not require much fertilizer, but a balanced fertilizer can be applied every 3-4 weeks during the growing season.

Harvesting: Cumin seeds are ready to harvest when the plant turns brown and the seeds turn brownish-black in color. Cut the seed heads from the plant and let them dry in a warm, dry place. Once dry, the seeds can be separated from the chaff and stored in an airtight container.

Currants

Currants are a type of berry that can be grown in raised beds. Here is some information on currant plant profiles for raised bed gardening:

Types of currants: There are several types of currants that can be grown in raised beds, including red currants, black currants, and white currants.

Soil requirements: Currants prefer well-draining soil that is slightly acidic with a pH between 6.0 and 6.5. Raised beds can be filled with a mix of garden soil, compost, and peat moss to create a suitable growing environment.

Sun and water requirements: Currants prefer full sun, but can tolerate partial shade. They need regular watering, especially during dry spells.

Planting and spacing: Currants should be planted in the spring, about 2-3 feet apart in rows spaced 6-8 feet apart. They should be planted at the same depth as they were in their nursery container.

Care and maintenance: Currants require regular pruning to maintain their shape and to remove any damaged or diseased wood. They should also be fertilized in the spring with a balanced fertilizer.

Harvesting: Currants are usually ready to harvest in late June to early July. The berries should be harvested when they are fully ripe, which can be determined by their color and texture. They can be eaten fresh or used in jams, jellies, and baked goods.

Dill

Dill (Anethum graveolens) is an annual herb that is commonly grown in raised bed gardens. It is a member of the Apiaceae family, which also includes carrots, parsley, and celery. Dill is prized for its feathery foliage, which has a distinctive aroma and flavor that is often used in pickling and seasoning dishes.

Dill grows best in well-drained soil that is rich in organic matter. It prefers full sun but can tolerate some shade. Dill plants should be spaced 12 to 18 inches apart in the raised bed, and they can reach a height of up to 3 feet.

Dill is easy to grow from seed, and it germinates quickly in warm soil. The seeds can be sown directly in the raised bed in early spring, or started indoors and transplanted once the seedlings have developed 2-3 true leaves.

Dill plants require regular watering, especially during hot, dry weather. However, care should be taken not to overwater, as this can lead to root rot. Dill is also prone to bolting, which means it will flower and produce seed prematurely if it becomes stressed. To prevent bolting, dill should be grown in soil that is evenly moist and fertilized regularly.

In addition to its culinary uses, dill has a number of medicinal benefits. It is believed to aid digestion, reduce inflammation, and improve sleep. Dill can also be used as a natural insect repellent in the garden, as its strong scent can help to deter pests.

Eggpolants

Eggplants are a popular vegetable to grow in a raised bed garden due to their compact size and high yields. Here's what you need to know about growing eggplants in your raised bed garden:

Varieties: There are many varieties of eggplants available, ranging in size, shape, and color. Popular varieties for raised bed gardens include 'Black Beauty', 'Ichiban', and 'Fairy Tale'.

Planting: Eggplants prefer warm, well-drained soil and should be planted in a raised bed with at least 6-8 hours of full sun per day. Seeds should be planted indoors 8-10 weeks before the last frost date, or seedlings can be planted directly into the raised bed after the danger of frost has passed.

Spacing: Eggplants should be spaced about 18-24 inches apart in the raised bed. If you're planting multiple rows, space the rows at least 24-36 inches apart to allow for adequate air circulation.

Watering: Eggplants require consistent moisture to thrive, so be sure to water them regularly, especially during hot, dry weather. Be careful not to overwater, as this can lead to root rot and other fungal diseases.

Fertilizing: Eggplants are heavy feeders and require regular fertilization throughout the growing season. Use a balanced, all-purpose fertilizer once a month or a slow-release fertilizer at the beginning of the growing season.

Harvesting: Eggplants should be harvested when they're firm and shiny, but before they become too large and tough. Use a sharp knife or pruning shears to cut the eggplant from the plant, being careful not to damage the stem.

Pests and Diseases: Eggplants are susceptible to a variety of pests and diseases, including flea beetles, aphids, and fungal diseases such as verticillium wilt and powdery mildew. To prevent these issues, be sure to keep your raised bed garden clean and well-maintained, and use organic pest control methods when necessary.

Figs

Figs (Ficus carica) are a sweet and juicy fruit that can be grown in raised beds. Here is some information about growing figs in raised beds:

Soil: Figs prefer well-draining soil that is rich in organic matter. Amend the soil in your raised bed with compost or well-rotted manure before planting.

Sunlight: Figs require full sun for at least 8 hours a day to produce fruit. Choose a location for your raised bed that receives plenty of sunlight.

Water: Figs require regular watering, especially during the growing season. Water deeply once a week, and more often during periods of drought.

Temperature: Figs are hardy in USDA zones 8-10 and can tolerate temperatures as low as 10°F. In colder climates, figs can be grown in containers and moved indoors during the winter.

Pruning: Figs should be pruned in late winter or early spring to remove any dead or diseased wood. Pinch back the tips of new growth to encourage branching and fruit production.

Varieties: Some popular fig varieties for home gardeners include 'Brown Turkey', 'Celeste', 'Chicago Hardy', and 'Black Mission'. Choose a variety that is suited to your climate and growing conditions.

Harvesting: Figs are ready to harvest when they are soft to the touch and the skin has turned a deep color. Pick the fruit gently to avoid bruising.

Garlic

Garlic is a flavorful and easy-to-grow crop that is well-suited to raised bed gardening. Here are some plant profiles for garlic in a raised bed garden:

Soil requirements: Garlic prefers loose, well-draining soil with a pH of 6.0 to 7.0. It's important to avoid soil that is too compact or heavy, as this can cause the bulbs to rot.

Planting: Garlic is typically planted in the fall, about 4-6 weeks before the first expected frost. Break apart the garlic bulbs into individual cloves, and plant them about 2-3 inches deep and 6 inches apart. Cover with soil, water well, and mulch to help conserve moisture.

Watering: Garlic needs consistent moisture, especially during the growing season. Water deeply once or twice a week, depending on weather conditions. Be sure to avoid overwatering, which can cause the bulbs to rot.

Fertilizing: Garlic doesn't require a lot of fertilizer, but a light application of balanced fertilizer or compost in the fall before planting can help provide the nutrients the bulbs need to grow.

Harvesting: Garlic is typically ready to harvest in mid- to late-summer, when the leaves start to turn brown and die back. Gently loosen the soil around the bulbs, being careful not to damage them, and pull them up by the stems. Allow the bulbs to dry in a cool, dry place for several weeks before storing.

Pests and diseases: Garlic is relatively pest-resistant, but can be susceptible to fungal diseases such as white rot and rust. Avoid planting garlic in the same spot two years in a row, and practice good crop rotation and sanitation practices to prevent the spread of disease.

Gooseberries

Gooseberries are an excellent choice for raised bed gardening as they are relatively easy to grow and maintain. They are a deciduous shrub that produces small, tart fruits that are high in Vitamin C. Here are some plant profiles for gooseberries:

Variety: Invicta

Description: Invicta gooseberries are a thornless variety that produces large, green-yellow fruits that are great for making jams and pies.

Growing requirements: Invicta gooseberries prefer full sun but can tolerate partial shade. They need well-draining soil and regular watering.

Variety: Hinnomaki Red

Description: Hinnomaki Red gooseberries produce medium-sized, red fruits that have a slightly sweeter flavor than other varieties.

Growing requirements: Hinnomaki Red gooseberries prefer full sun but can tolerate partial shade. They need well-draining soil and regular watering.

Variety: Pixwell

Description: Pixwell gooseberries produce small, green fruits that are great for snacking or making preserves.

Growing requirements: Pixwell gooseberries prefer full sun but can tolerate partial shade. They need well-draining soil and regular watering.

Variety: Captivator

Description: Captivator gooseberries produce large, sweet fruits that are great for eating fresh or making desserts.

Growing requirements: Captivator gooseberries prefer full sun but can tolerate partial shade. They need well-draining soil and regular watering.

Green Beans

Green beans are a popular and easy-to-grow vegetable that can thrive in a raised bed garden. Here are some key plant profile details to consider when growing green beans in your raised bed:

Planting: Green beans can be planted directly in the raised bed garden once the soil has warmed up in the spring. They prefer well-drained soil with a pH between 6.0 and 7.5. Sow the seeds about 1 inch deep and 2-3 inches apart, and water well. You can also plant seedlings that have been started indoors.

Sunlight: Green beans need full sun to grow properly, so be sure to choose a spot in your raised bed that gets at least 6-8 hours of direct sunlight per day.

Watering: Green beans need regular watering, especially during hot and dry weather. Water deeply once or twice a week, depending on the weather conditions.

Fertilizing: Green beans don't need much fertilizer, but you can add a balanced fertilizer (such as 10-10-10) to the soil before planting to help promote healthy growth. Avoid using high-nitrogen fertilizers, as they can encourage leafy growth at the expense of bean production.

Mulching: Mulching around your green bean plants can help conserve moisture, regulate soil temperature, and suppress weeds. Use a layer of organic mulch such as straw, grass clippings, or shredded leaves.

Support: Green beans are climbing plants and will need support to grow properly. You can use trellises, stakes, or a bean tower to keep the plants off the ground and encourage better air circulation.

Harvesting: Green beans are ready to harvest about 50-60 days after planting. Look for beans that are firm, crisp, and about the size of a pencil. Pick them regularly to encourage continued production. If you allow the beans to grow too large, they will become tough and stringy.

Kale

Kale is a leafy green vegetable that is easy to grow in a raised bed garden. Here are some plant profiles for kale to help you get started:

Soil requirements: Kale prefers well-drained soil that is rich in organic matter. The soil pH should be between 6.0 and 7.0.

Sun requirements: Kale prefers full sun but can tolerate some shade.

Water requirements: Kale needs regular watering to thrive. Be sure to water deeply and frequently, especially during dry spells.

Planting: Kale can be grown from seed or transplants. Seeds should be sown ½ inch deep and 12-18 inches apart. Transplants should be planted at the same depth they were in their containers, and spaced 12-18 inches apart.

Maintenance: Kale is a relatively low-maintenance plant. Fertilize with a balanced fertilizer every 4-6 weeks, and be sure to keep the soil moist.

Harvesting: Kale can be harvested as soon as the leaves are large enough to use. Simply cut the outer leaves from the plant, leaving the inner leaves to continue growing. Kale can be harvested throughout the growing season.

Pests and diseases: Kale is relatively resistant to pests and diseases, but can be susceptible to aphids, cabbage worms, and powdery mildew. Keep an eye out for any signs of damage, and take action as needed to protect your plants.

Honeyberries

Honeyberries, also known as haskap or edible honeysuckle, are a delicious and nutritious berry that is becoming increasingly popular in North America. They are a great addition to any raised bed garden as they are easy to grow and require very little maintenance. Here are some plant profiles for honeyberries:

Variety: Borealis

Description: A high-yielding honeyberry cultivar that produces large, sweet berries. It is known for its hardiness and disease resistance.

Growing conditions: Borealis prefers well-draining soil that is rich in organic matter. It can tolerate partial shade but produces better in full sun. It is also cold-hardy and can withstand temperatures as low as -40°C.

Harvest season: Mid to late June.

Variety: Tundra

Description: Tundra is a compact honeyberry bush that produces medium-sized, sweet berries. It is a hardy cultivar that is resistant to common honeyberry diseases.

Growing conditions: Tundra prefers well-draining soil and can tolerate a wide range of soil types. It requires full sun to produce the best yields. It is also very cold-hardy and can withstand temperatures as low as -45°C.

Harvest season: Early to mid-June.

Variety: Aurora

Description: Aurora is a large honeyberry cultivar that produces large, sweet berries. It is known for its early ripening and high yield.

Growing conditions: Aurora prefers well-draining soil that is rich in organic matter. It can tolerate partial shade but produces better in full sun. It is also cold-hardy and can withstand temperatures as low as -45°C.

Harvest season: Late May to early June.

Honeydew Melon

Honeydew melons are a sweet and juicy fruit that can be grown in raised beds. Here are some plant profile details for honeydew melons:

Sunlight: Honeydew melons need full sunlight, so choose a spot in your raised bed that gets at least 6-8 hours of direct sunlight each day.

Soil: Melons prefer well-drained soil that is rich in organic matter. A pH range of 6.0 to 6.8 is ideal.

Watering: Honeydew melons need regular watering to keep the soil moist but not waterlogged. Water deeply once a week, or more often in hot, dry weather.

Temperature: Honeydew melons thrive in warm weather with daytime temperatures between 70-85°F. If temperatures exceed 90°F, the fruit may become sunburned.

Fertilizer: Melons are heavy feeders and require regular fertilization. Use a balanced fertilizer that is high in nitrogen during the vegetative stage, and then switch to a fertilizer that is higher in phosphorus and potassium once the fruit begins to form.

Pests and diseases: Melons can be susceptible to a number of pests and diseases, including cucumber beetles, aphids, powdery mildew, and Fusarium wilt. Monitor your plants regularly and take action at the first sign of infestation or disease.

Harvesting: Honeydew melons are ready to harvest when the skin turns a creamy yellow color and the fruit develops a sweet fragrance. Gently press the end opposite the stem, and if it gives slightly, the melon is ripe. Cut the fruit from the vine with a sharp knife or scissors.

Leeks

Leeks are a versatile and flavorful vegetable that are well-suited for raised bed gardening. Here's a profile of this delicious plant:

Plant type: Leeks are a member of the allium family, which includes onions, garlic, and shallots. They grow as long, cylindrical stalks with a mild, onion-like flavor.

Growing season: Leeks are a cool-season crop that are typically planted in the fall or early spring. They take a long time to mature, with some varieties taking up to 120 days to reach full size.

Soil requirements: Leeks prefer a well-draining soil that is rich in organic matter. They also require a soil pH of 6.0 to 7.0.

Light requirements: Leeks prefer full sun, but can tolerate some shade.

Water requirements: Leeks require consistent moisture to grow properly. Water deeply and regularly, especially during dry spells.

Fertilizer requirements: Leeks are heavy feeders and require regular fertilization throughout the growing season. Use a balanced fertilizer and follow the manufacturer's instructions for application rates.

Pest and disease control: Leeks are susceptible to a variety of pests and diseases, including thrips, onion maggots, and rust. Practice good garden hygiene, such as removing diseased plants, to minimize the risk of infection. Consider using row covers to protect young plants from pests.

Harvesting: Leeks are ready to harvest when they reach a diameter of at least 1 inch. To harvest, gently pull the plant out of the soil and cut off the roots and the dark green leaves. Store harvested leeks in a cool, dry place for up to a week.

Uses: Leeks are a versatile ingredient that can be used in a variety of dishes, such as soups, stews, and casseroles. They can also be sautéed or roasted and served as a side dish.

Lemongrass

Lemongrass (Cymbopogon citratus) is a tropical herb that is commonly used in Asian cuisine for its lemony flavor and aroma. It's a great addition to a raised bed garden because it can tolerate a wide range of soil conditions and requires little maintenance.

Here are some plant profile details for lemongrass:

Light requirements: Lemongrass needs full sun to thrive, so make sure it's planted in a location that gets at least 6-8 hours of direct sunlight per day.

Water requirements: Lemongrass prefers consistently moist soil but can also tolerate some drought. Water deeply once or twice a week, depending on the weather and soil conditions.

Soil requirements: Lemongrass prefers well-draining soil with a slightly acidic pH (between 6.0 and 7.5). If your soil is heavy and clay-like, consider adding compost or sand to improve drainage.

Temperature requirements: Lemongrass is a tropical plant that prefers warm temperatures between 70-95°F (21-35°C). It can't tolerate frost or freezing temperatures, so it's best to grow it in a raised bed or container that can be moved indoors during the winter.

Harvesting: To harvest lemongrass, wait until the stalks are at least 1/2 inch in diameter and 12-18 inches tall. Cut the stalks as close to the ground as possible, leaving about 2 inches of the base intact. You can use the stalks fresh, dried, or frozen for later use.

Companion planting: Lemongrass can be planted with other herbs and vegetables such as basil, mint, tomatoes, and peppers. It can also help repel pests such as mosquitoes, ants, and aphids.

Lettuce

Lettuce is a popular and easy-to-grow crop in a raised bed garden. Here are some important things to know about growing lettuce:

Soil: Lettuce prefers a loose, well-draining soil that is rich in organic matter. A soil mix of compost, peat moss, and vermiculite or perlite is ideal.

Sunlight: Lettuce prefers partial shade, especially during the hottest parts of the day. In a raised bed garden, this can be achieved by planting lettuce under taller crops or using shade cloth.

Watering: Lettuce needs consistent moisture, so it's important to water it regularly. A drip irrigation system or soaker hose can help ensure that the soil stays evenly moist.

Temperature: Lettuce prefers cooler temperatures, with an optimal range of 60-65°F. In hot weather, lettuce may bolt, or go to seed, which can make the leaves bitter and tough.

Planting: Lettuce can be planted in spring or fall. In spring, plant lettuce seeds as soon as the soil can be worked. In fall, plant lettuce seeds 6-8 weeks before the first expected frost.

Harvesting: Lettuce can be harvested when the leaves are large enough to eat. Harvest individual leaves as needed, or cut the entire plant at once. To keep lettuce fresh, store it in a plastic bag in the refrigerator.

Varieties: There are many different varieties of lettuce to choose from, including leaf lettuce, romaine lettuce, and butterhead lettuce. Some popular varieties include 'Black Seeded Simpson', 'Green Oakleaf', and 'Buttercrunch'.

Levander

Lavender is a popular herb known for its beautiful purple flowers, soothing fragrance, and medicinal properties. It's a great addition to any garden, including raised beds.

Here are some key plant profile information for growing lavender in raised beds:

Soil and Sunlight Requirements: Lavender requires well-drained soil with a pH of 6.5 to 7.5. It also needs full sunlight to grow properly.

Planting Time: Lavender can be planted in spring or fall.

Planting Depth and Spacing: When planting lavender in raised beds, dig a hole that is twice as wide and deep as the root ball. Space plants about 12 to 18 inches apart.

Watering: Lavender prefers dry soil, so avoid over-watering. Water deeply once a week during the growing season and let the soil dry out before watering again.

Fertilizing: Lavender doesn't require a lot of fertilization. You can add compost or a slow-release fertilizer in the spring.

Pruning: To keep lavender plants looking neat and healthy, prune them back by one-third in the spring.

Harvesting: Harvest lavender flowers just as they begin to open. Cut the stems just above the leaves and hang them upside down to dry.

Licorice

Licorice (Glycyrrhiza glabra) is a perennial herb that can be grown in raised beds for its medicinal and culinary properties. Here are some plant profiles for licorice:

Growing requirements: Licorice prefers full sun to partial shade and well-drained soil. It can grow up to 5 feet tall and requires a deep, wide container to accommodate its long taproot. Licorice plants also require consistent moisture, so make sure to water them regularly.

Propagation: Licorice can be propagated through root cuttings or seeds. Root cuttings should be taken in the fall or early spring and planted directly in the garden bed or container. Seeds can be started indoors 6-8 weeks before the last frost and transplanted outside when the seedlings are 4-6 inches tall.

Harvesting: The roots of licorice plants are harvested in the fall of the plant's third or fourth year. To harvest, carefully dig up the root system and remove the outer layer of bark to reveal the sweet, woody interior. The roots can be dried and used in teas, tinctures, or as a natural sweetener.

Companion planting: Licorice can be grown alongside other herbs such as mint, thyme, and basil. It is also a good companion plant for vegetables such as tomatoes, peppers, and eggplants.

Benefits: Licorice has been used for centuries for its medicinal properties, including its ability to soothe sore throats, relieve coughs, and ease digestive issues. It is also a natural sweetener and can be used as a substitute for sugar in recipes.

Majoram

Marjoram is a fragrant herb that belongs to the mint family. It is native to the Mediterranean region and is commonly used in Mediterranean and Middle Eastern cuisine. Marjoram has a sweet, slightly bitter flavor and is often used to flavor meat dishes, soups, stews, and sauces.

When grown in a raised bed, marjoram requires well-draining soil and plenty of sunlight. It can be grown from seeds or transplanted seedlings. Marjoram plants prefer temperatures between 60 and 70 degrees Fahrenheit and should be watered regularly, but not overwatered.

Marjoram is a low-maintenance plant and can be harvested throughout the growing season. The leaves can be harvested when the plant reaches a height of 6 to 8 inches. To harvest, simply snip off the leaves at the stem. Marjoram leaves can be used fresh or dried, and can be stored in an airtight container for later use.

In addition to its culinary uses, marjoram is also used for its medicinal properties. It has been used to treat a variety of ailments, including digestive issues, headaches, and anxiety. However, it is important to consult with a healthcare professional before using marjoram for medicinal purposes.

Mint

Mint is a popular herb known for its refreshing scent and flavor. It is easy to grow in raised bed gardens and can thrive in both sunny and shady locations.

Mint plants prefer well-draining soil that is moist but not waterlogged. They also require regular watering and benefit from occasional fertilization.

There are many different varieties of mint, including peppermint, spearmint, and chocolate mint. Each type has its own unique flavor and can be used in a variety of recipes.

Mint is often used in teas, cocktails, and desserts, but it can also be added to savory dishes such as salads, soups, and marinades. It is also a great addition to homemade cleaning products and can help to repel insects.

While mint is a resilient plant, it can become invasive if not properly contained. To prevent this, it is recommended to grow mint in a container or to plant it in a raised bed with a barrier to keep the roots from spreading.

Okra

Okra (Abelmoschus esculentus) is a warm-season vegetable that is widely grown in Southern United States, India, and other tropical and subtropical regions around the world. It is a member of the mallow family, which also includes hibiscus and cotton.

Here are some plant profile details for Okra:

Soil Requirements: Okra prefers well-drained soil that is rich in organic matter. The soil should be slightly acidic with a pH between 6.0 and 6.5.

Sun Exposure: Okra plants require full sun for optimal growth and production. They should be planted in a location that receives at least six hours of direct sunlight per day.

Watering: Okra plants need regular watering, especially during hot, dry weather. It is best to water deeply once or twice a week, rather than shallowly and frequently.

Temperature and Humidity: Okra plants require warm temperatures to grow and produce fruit. They do not tolerate frost or temperatures below 50°F. Okra also prefers high humidity levels, so it is important to keep the soil moist and to avoid letting the plants dry out.

Fertilizing: Okra plants benefit from regular fertilization, especially during the growing season. A balanced fertilizer with a higher amount of phosphorus (P) and potassium (K) is recommended.

Pests and Diseases: Okra plants are susceptible to a range of pests and diseases, including aphids, spider mites, fruit worms, and root knot nematodes. Regular monitoring and treatment with organic or chemical controls may be necessary.

Harvesting: Okra pods are ready to harvest when they are 2-4 inches long and still tender. They should be picked regularly to encourage continued production. Okra pods can be used fresh or cooked in a variety of dishes, including stews, soups, and fried dishes.

Onions

Onions are a great addition to any raised bed garden. Here's what you need to know about growing them:

Planting: Onions can be planted as seeds or sets (small bulbs). If planting from seed, start them indoors 6-8 weeks before your last frost date. Plant the seeds 1/4 inch deep and keep them moist. When the seedlings are about 6 inches tall, transplant them into your raised bed garden, spacing them 4-6 inches apart. If using sets, plant them directly in your garden, burying them about 1 inch deep and spacing them 4-6 inches apart.

Soil: Onions prefer well-drained soil that is high in organic matter. Before planting, amend your soil with compost or well-rotted manure to improve its texture and fertility.

Sun and water: Onions need full sun and regular watering, especially during dry spells. Be sure to water deeply, but avoid over-watering, as this can lead to rot.

Fertilizer: Onions benefit from a balanced fertilizer high in nitrogen. Apply fertilizer in the spring when the plants are about 6 inches tall, and again in mid-summer.

Mulching: Mulch around the base of your onion plants to help retain moisture and suppress weeds.

Harvesting: Onions are ready to harvest when the tops start to yellow and fall over. Gently lift the onions out of the ground and allow them to dry in the sun for a few days. Once they're dry, trim the tops and roots and store the onions in a cool, dry place.

Oregano

Oregano is a popular herb that is commonly used in Mediterranean and Mexican cuisine. It is easy to grow and maintain, making it an ideal plant for raised bed gardening. Here are some plant profiles for oregano:

Plant type: Perennial herb

Soil and sunlight requirements: Oregano prefers well-drained soil with a pH range of 6.0 to 8.0. It grows best in full sun, but can also tolerate partial shade.

Water requirements: Oregano requires moderate watering, but make sure not to overwater it. Allow the soil to dry out between watering.

Planting time: Oregano can be planted in the spring or fall.

Planting method: Plant oregano seeds or cuttings in well-drained soil, about 6-8 inches apart. Make sure to plant them at the same depth they were in their original pot.

Maintenance: Oregano requires minimal maintenance. Keep the soil moist and weed around the plants regularly. Cut back the stems to promote bushy growth and to prevent them from becoming woody.

Harvesting: Oregano leaves can be harvested when the plant is about 6 inches tall. Cut the stems with sharp scissors or pruning shears, leaving at least 2 inches of stem. Harvest oregano in the morning, after the dew has dried but before the heat of the day.

Parnsnips

Parsnips are a popular root vegetable that can be grown in a raised bed garden. Here are some key plant profile details:

Soil and water requirements: Parsnips prefer well-draining, fertile soil that is rich in organic matter. They require consistent moisture, so be sure to water regularly and deeply.

Sun requirements: Parsnips require full sun exposure to thrive. Plant them in a location that receives at least 6-8 hours of direct sunlight each day.

Planting time: Parsnips are a cool-season crop and should be planted in early spring, as soon as the soil can be worked. They can also be planted in late summer for a fall harvest.

Spacing: When planting parsnips in a raised bed garden, space them 3-4 inches apart in rows that are 12-18 inches apart.

Growing tips: Parsnips are slow-growing and can take up to 120 days to mature, so be patient. To encourage straight root growth, make sure the soil is well-drained and free of rocks or debris. Mulch around the plants to help retain moisture and control weeds.

Harvesting: Parsnips are ready to harvest when they reach their full size, which can range from 6-12 inches long and 2-3 inches in diameter. Use a garden fork or spade to carefully lift the parsnips from the soil. They can be stored in a cool, dry place for several months.

Pests and diseases: Parsnips are relatively pest and disease-resistant, but can be susceptible to root rot and leaf spot. Rotate your crops each year to help prevent these issues.

Parsley

Parsley (Petroselinum crispum) is a popular herb used in cooking and garnishing. It is a biennial plant that can grow up to 30 cm in height and prefers well-draining soil in full sun or partial shade.

Parsley is known for its distinct flat or curly leaves, which are rich in vitamins A, C, and K, as well as iron and potassium. The leaves can be harvested throughout the growing season and used fresh or dried.

In addition to its culinary uses, parsley has a long history of medicinal use. It is believed to have diuretic properties and may help with digestion, respiratory issues, and inflammation.

When planting parsley, it is best to start with seeds rather than transplants, as parsley has a long taproot that can be easily disturbed. The seeds should be planted in moist soil and kept well-watered until they germinate.

Peas

Peas are a popular vegetable to grow in a raised bed garden because they are relatively easy to grow, have a high yield, and are very nutritious. Here are some plant profiles for peas in a raised bed garden:

Varieties: There are two main types of peas to consider when planting in a raised bed garden: shelling peas and sugar snap peas. Shelling peas are typically eaten when they are still in the pod but have fully matured, while sugar snap peas are eaten whole, including the pod. Some popular varieties of shelling peas include Lincoln and Little Marvel, while popular sugar snap pea varieties include Sugar Ann and Sugar Daddy.

Planting: Peas should be planted in the early spring, as soon as the soil can be worked. They prefer cool weather and will stop producing pods once the temperature gets too warm. Plant the seeds about 1 inch deep and 2-3 inches apart, and provide support for the plants to climb as they grow.

Care: Peas are relatively low-maintenance, but they do require some care to ensure a healthy harvest. Water regularly, especially during dry periods, and mulch around the base of the plants to help retain moisture. Fertilize once or twice during the growing season with a balanced fertilizer.

Harvest: Peas are typically ready to harvest about 60-70 days after planting. Shelling peas should be picked when the pods are plump and full but before they start to dry out. Sugar snap peas can be picked when the pods are fully formed but still tender and crisp.

Pests and diseases: Peas are relatively resistant to pests and diseases, but they can be susceptible to powdery mildew and aphids. Keep an eye out for any signs of damage or disease, and take action as needed to protect your plants.

Potatoes

Potatoes are a versatile and easy-to-grow crop that can be a great addition to your raised bed garden. Here are some plant profile tips to help you successfully grow potatoes in your raised bed:

Soil preparation: Potatoes grow best in loose, well-draining soil that is rich in organic matter. Before planting, amend your soil with compost or aged manure to improve its texture and nutrient content. Potatoes also prefer a slightly acidic soil with a pH between 5.0 and 6.0.

Planting: Plant seed potatoes (small potatoes that have been allowed to sprout) in late winter or early spring, as soon as the soil can be worked. Cut the seed potatoes into chunks, making sure each chunk has at least one "eye" (the sprout). Plant the chunks 4-6 inches deep, spaced 12-18 inches apart in rows that are 2-3 feet apart. As the plants grow, mound soil up around the stems to prevent the developing tubers from being exposed to sunlight and turning green.

Watering: Potatoes need consistent moisture to produce a good crop. Water deeply once or twice a week, or more often during hot, dry weather. Avoid overhead watering, which can encourage disease.

Fertilizing: Potatoes are heavy feeders and benefit from regular fertilization. Apply a balanced fertilizer, such as 10-10-10, at planting time, and again when the plants are 6-8 inches tall. Avoid high-nitrogen fertilizers, which can result in lush foliage but few tubers.

Harvesting: Potatoes are ready to harvest when the plants begin to die back and the foliage turns yellow. Gently dig around the plants with a garden fork to loosen the soil, then carefully lift out the potatoes. Be sure to handle them gently to avoid bruising or damage. Allow the harvested potatoes to dry in a cool, dark place for a week or two before storing.

Pumpkins

Pumpkins are a popular choice for raised bed gardening due to their large, sprawling vines and colorful, nutritious fruit. Here are some key plant profile details for growing pumpkins in a raised bed:

Soil requirements: Pumpkins prefer well-draining soil with a pH between 6.0 and 7.0. Raised beds can be filled with a mixture of topsoil, compost, and perlite to provide good drainage.

Sun requirements: Pumpkins need full sun to thrive, so choose a location in your raised bed that gets at least 6-8 hours of direct sunlight per day.

Planting: Sow pumpkin seeds directly into the raised bed after all danger of frost has passed, or start seeds indoors 2-4 weeks before the last frost date and transplant seedlings into the bed once they have several true leaves.

Spacing: Pumpkins need plenty of room to spread out, so plant them about 4-6 feet apart in the raised bed.

Watering: Pumpkins need consistent moisture to grow, so water deeply once or twice a week, depending on the weather and soil conditions.

Fertilizing: Pumpkins are heavy feeders and benefit from regular applications of organic fertilizer or compost throughout the growing season.

Harvesting: Pumpkins are ready to harvest when the stem turns brown and the fruit has reached its full color. Cut the fruit off the vine, leaving a few inches of stem attached, and store in a cool, dry place for several weeks to cure before using.

Radishes

Radishes are a popular vegetable to grow in raised bed gardens due to their quick growing time and easy-to-grow nature. Here are some plant profiles for radishes in raised bed gardens:

Soil: Radishes prefer loose, well-draining soil that is rich in organic matter. A pH of 6.0 to 7.0 is ideal for radishes. Raised bed gardens can provide the perfect environment for radishes, as the loose soil allows for good drainage and aeration.

Sunlight: Radishes need full sun to grow properly. They require at least 6 hours of direct sunlight per day. Raised bed gardens should be placed in a location that receives full sun throughout the day.

Watering: Radishes prefer consistent moisture, but overwatering can cause the roots to split. Water the plants deeply once or twice a week, depending on the weather conditions. Raised bed gardens should be watered from the base to avoid wetting the leaves, which can lead to fungal disease.

Temperature: Radishes grow best in cool weather. They prefer temperatures between 50°F and 65°F. In warm weather, radishes will bolt and become tough and woody. Raised bed gardens can be covered with shade cloth to protect the plants from excessive heat.

Planting: Radish seeds should be planted directly in the raised bed garden soil, about 1/2 inch deep and 1 inch apart. Radishes can be planted in the early spring or fall for the best results. Raised bed gardens can be prepared with a layer of compost before planting to provide nutrients for the growing plants.

Pests and Diseases: Radishes are generally resistant to pests and diseases, but they can be attacked by root maggots and flea beetles. To prevent these pests, cover the raised bed garden with row covers or insect netting. Diseases such as damping off and powdery mildew can be prevented by providing good air circulation and avoiding overwatering.

Harvesting: Radishes are ready to harvest in about 3 to 4 weeks after planting. They should be harvested when they reach the desired size, as leaving them in the ground too long can cause them to become woody and bitter. Use a garden fork or your hands to gently pull the radishes from the soil.

Raspberries

Raspberries are delicious and nutritious fruits that can be grown in raised bed gardens. Here are some plant profiles for raspberries:

Variety: There are two types of raspberries: summer-bearing and fall-bearing. Summer-bearing raspberries produce fruit once a year in the summer, while fall-bearing raspberries produce fruit twice a year, once in the summer and once in the fall. Some popular summer-bearing varieties include 'Heritage,' 'Latham,' and 'Canby,' while popular fall-bearing varieties include 'Autumn Bliss' and 'Heritage.'

Soil: Raspberries prefer well-draining soil that is rich in organic matter. Raised beds can be filled with a mixture of compost, peat moss, and perlite to create an ideal growing environment for raspberries.

Planting: Raspberries should be planted in the spring or fall. Space plants 2-3 feet apart in rows that are 6-8 feet apart. Plant the canes so that the soil line is just below the surface of the soil.

Care: Raspberries require regular watering, especially during the fruiting season. Mulch around the plants to conserve moisture and suppress weeds. Raspberries should be fertilized in the spring and again after the fruiting season is over. Prune the canes in the fall or winter to remove old or damaged wood.

Harvest: Raspberries are ready to harvest when they are fully ripe and easily come off the plant. Pick the berries regularly to encourage the plant to produce more fruit. Raspberries can be eaten fresh, frozen, or used in jams, jellies, and baked goods.

Rosemary

Rosemary (Rosmarinus officinalis) is a fragrant, evergreen herb that is commonly used in cooking and herbal medicine. It is a hardy perennial that can be grown in raised beds and containers, making it a great choice for home gardeners who have limited space.

Here are some key plant profile details for rosemary:

Soil Requirements: Rosemary prefers well-draining, slightly acidic soil with a pH of 6.0 to 7.0. It can tolerate sandy or loamy soil, but does not like heavy clay soil. To improve soil drainage, you can add compost or perlite to your raised bed.

Sun Exposure: Rosemary needs full sun to thrive. It should be planted in a location that gets at least six hours of direct sunlight each day.

Watering: Rosemary is drought-tolerant and does not require frequent watering. In fact, overwatering can cause root rot. Water your rosemary plant deeply once a week during the growing season, and reduce watering in the winter.

Fertilizer: Rosemary does not require a lot of fertilizer, but a light application of organic fertilizer in the spring can help it grow better. Avoid using chemical fertilizers, as they can damage the plant.

Pruning: Rosemary should be pruned regularly to maintain its shape and encourage new growth. You can prune the plant at any time, but it is best to do so in the spring before new growth starts.

Harvesting: Rosemary leaves can be harvested at any time, but the best time is in the morning when the essential oils are most concentrated. To harvest, simply snip off a few sprigs from the plant.

Rhubarb

Rhubarb is a popular perennial vegetable that can be grown in a raised bed garden. Here are some plant profiles for growing rhubarb:

Soil Requirements: Rhubarb prefers well-drained, fertile soil with a pH between 5.5 and 6.8. Before planting, amend the soil with organic matter, such as compost or well-rotted manure.

Sun Requirements: Rhubarb prefers full sun, but can tolerate some shade.

Planting: Rhubarb can be planted in the spring or fall. Plant the crowns (the root and stem portion) about 2 inches below the soil surface, with the growing tips just above the soil. Space the plants about 3 feet apart.

Watering: Rhubarb requires consistent moisture, especially during hot, dry periods. Water deeply once a week, or more often during hot weather.

Fertilizing: Rhubarb benefits from a balanced fertilizer in the spring, and a top dressing of compost or well-rotted manure in the fall.

Harvesting: Rhubarb can be harvested in the second year after planting. Pull the stalks gently from the base of the plant, twisting slightly as you pull. Be sure to leave a few stalks on the plant to ensure continued growth.

Pests and Diseases: Rhubarb is generally resistant to pests and diseases, but can be affected by crown rot or powdery mildew. To prevent these issues, avoid planting in poorly-drained soil and water at the base of the plant rather than overhead.

Sage

Sage, also known as Salvia officinalis, is a popular herb that is commonly used in cooking and for medicinal purposes. It is a perennial plant that is native to the Mediterranean region and is often grown in herb gardens.

Sage plants can grow up to 2-3 feet tall and wide, and have oblong, gray-green leaves that are highly aromatic. In the summer, the plant produces small, tubular, purple or blue flowers that are attractive to bees and butterflies.

Sage is a hardy plant that prefers full sun and well-draining soil. It is drought-tolerant and does not require a lot of water once established. It is also a low-maintenance plant that does not require fertilization or pruning.

In the kitchen, sage is a versatile herb that is often used in poultry, sausage, and stuffing recipes. It has a slightly bitter, earthy flavor that complements rich meats and savory dishes. It can also be used to make teas and tinctures for medicinal purposes.

Sage is believed to have several health benefits, including improving digestion, reducing inflammation, and enhancing cognitive function. It contains compounds that have antioxidant and antimicrobial properties, making it a popular herb for natural remedies.

Savory Tarragon

Savory tarragon (Artemisia dracunculus) is a perennial herb that is commonly used in French cuisine. It is a member of the Asteraceae family and is native to Europe and Asia. In raised bed gardening, it is a great addition as it doesn't take up a lot of space and is easy to care for.

Here are some plant profile details for savory tarragon:

Growing Conditions: Savory tarragon prefers full sun and well-draining soil. It can tolerate some shade, but its growth may be stunted. The plant likes to be kept consistently moist, but not waterlogged.

Planting: Savory tarragon can be grown from seeds or cuttings. If planting from seed, it is best to start indoors in early spring and then transplant the seedlings outside after the last frost. Cuttings can be taken in the spring or fall and rooted in water or soil.

Maintenance: Savory tarragon is a low-maintenance plant. It does not require fertilization and can be pruned as needed to promote bushier growth. The plant is not very drought-tolerant, so it should be watered regularly.

Harvesting: The leaves of savory tarragon can be harvested throughout the growing season. They are best used fresh, but can also be dried and stored for later use. The flavor of the leaves is strongest just before the plant flowers.

Companion Plants: Savory tarragon pairs well with other herbs such as basil, parsley, and chives. It can also be planted alongside vegetables like tomatoes, peppers, and eggplants.

Shallots

Shallots are a member of the onion family and are often grown for their flavorful and aromatic bulbs. They are a popular ingredient in many culinary dishes, including French cuisine, and are easy to grow in a raised bed garden.

Here are some plant profile details for shallots:

Planting: Shallots should be planted in the fall or early spring. They prefer a well-drained soil with plenty of organic matter. Plant each bulb about 4-6 inches apart and 1-2 inches deep, with the pointy end facing up.

Sunlight: Shallots require full sun exposure to grow well.

Watering: Shallots prefer moist soil, but it's important not to overwater them. Water the plants deeply once or twice a week, depending on the weather.

Fertilizing: Shallots are not heavy feeders, but they can benefit from a balanced fertilizer applied once a month during the growing season.

Harvesting: Shallots are ready to harvest when the tops begin to turn yellow and fall over. Carefully dig them up with a fork, being careful not to damage the bulbs. Allow them to cure for a week or two in a cool, dry, and well-ventilated area before storing them.

Pests and Diseases: Shallots are generally resistant to pests and diseases, but they can be affected by onion maggots and thrips. Avoid planting shallots in the same location as other alliums, such as onions and garlic, to prevent the buildup of soil-borne diseases.

Uses: Shallots can be used in a variety of dishes, including soups, stews, and stir-fries. They are often used to add flavor to sauces, dressings, and marinades. They have a milder and sweeter taste compared to onions and can be a great substitute for those who find onions too strong.

Spinach

Spinach is a nutritious and easy-to-grow leafy green that is well-suited for raised bed gardening. Here's what you need to know to successfully grow spinach in your raised bed:

Soil: Spinach prefers well-draining soil with a pH between 6.0 and 7.0. Raised beds filled with a high-quality soil mix that has plenty of organic matter are ideal for growing spinach.

Sunlight: Spinach prefers partial shade to full sun. In hot climates, it's best to plant spinach in a location that receives morning sun and afternoon shade.

Water: Spinach requires consistent moisture to thrive. Be sure to water your plants deeply once or twice a week, depending on the weather and the soil moisture level.

Planting: Spinach can be direct-seeded into your raised bed in early spring or late summer. Sow the seeds 1/2 inch deep and 2-4 inches apart, and cover lightly with soil. Spinach can also be started indoors and transplanted into your raised bed when the plants are 2-3 inches tall.

Fertilizer: Spinach benefits from regular fertilization with a balanced fertilizer, such as a 10-10-10 or 12-12-12 blend. Be sure to follow the instructions on the package and avoid over-fertilizing, as this can lead to leafy growth at the expense of the roots.

Pests and Diseases: Spinach can be susceptible to pests such as aphids and leaf miners, as well as diseases such as downy mildew and leaf spot. To prevent these problems, be sure to keep your raised bed clean and weed-free, and avoid overcrowding your plants.

Harvesting: Spinach can be harvested when the leaves are large enough to use, typically 30-45 days after planting. Harvest the leaves by cutting them off at the base of the plant, being careful not to damage the remaining leaves. Spinach can be harvested continuously throughout the growing season, but it's best to avoid harvesting more than one-third of the leaves at a time to avoid stressing the plants.

Squash

Squash is a warm-weather vegetable that thrives in the well-drained soil of a raised bed garden. There are many different types of squash to choose from, including summer squash, zucchini, and winter squash, each with their own unique characteristics.

When growing squash in your raised bed garden, here are some plant profiles to keep in mind:

Summer squash: Summer squash, such as yellow squash and zucchini, are quick-growing vegetables that are easy to grow in a raised bed garden. They prefer warm soil temperatures and should be planted in the spring once the soil has warmed up. Summer squash plants are very prolific, so be prepared for a bumper crop.

Zucchini: Zucchini is a type of summer squash that's easy to grow and produces a lot of fruit. It's best to harvest zucchini when they're young and tender, as they can become tough and bitter if left on the vine for too long. Zucchini plants are also susceptible to powdery mildew, so be sure to keep an eye out for any signs of this fungal disease.

Winter squash: Winter squash, such as butternut squash and acorn squash, are slower-growing vegetables that require a longer growing season. They're typically planted in the early summer and harvested in the fall. Winter squash plants can take up a lot of space in your raised bed garden, so be sure to give them plenty of room to grow.

Butternut squash: Butternut squash is a type of winter squash that's easy to grow and produces a lot of fruit. It's best to harvest butternut squash when they're fully mature and the skin is hard and difficult to pierce with your fingernail. Butternut squash plants are also susceptible to squash vine borers, so be sure to keep an eye out for any signs of this destructive pest.

Acorn squash: Acorn squash is a type of winter squash that's smaller than butternut squash but still produces a lot of fruit. It's best to harvest acorn squash when they're fully mature and the skin is hard and difficult to pierce with your fingernail. Acorn squash plants are also susceptible to squash bugs, so be sure to keep an eye out for any signs of this pest.

Strawberries

Strawberries are a delicious and nutritious fruit that can be easily grown in raised beds. Here are some plant profiles for strawberries:

Varieties: There are three types of strawberries: June-bearing, everbearing, and day-neutral. June-bearing strawberries produce a single crop in late spring or early summer, while everbearing strawberries produce two crops, one in late spring and one in early fall. Day-neutral strawberries produce fruit throughout the growing season.

Soil requirements: Strawberries prefer well-drained, slightly acidic soil with a pH between 5.5 and 6.5. It is important to amend the soil with organic matter such as compost or well-rotted manure before planting.

Sunlight requirements: Strawberries require full sun to produce a good crop. Make sure to choose a location for your raised bed that receives at least six hours of direct sunlight per day.

Planting: Strawberry plants should be planted in early spring, as soon as the soil can be worked. Space plants 12-18 inches apart in rows that are 2-3 feet apart. Make sure to plant the crown of the plant at soil level and water well after planting.

Care: Keep the soil consistently moist throughout the growing season. Apply a layer of mulch around the plants to help retain moisture and suppress weeds. Fertilize with a balanced fertilizer in the spring and again in the fall.

Harvesting: Strawberries should be harvested when they are fully ripe, which is when they are fully red and slightly soft to the touch. Pick strawberries regularly to encourage the plant to produce more fruit.

Pests and diseases: Common pests that affect strawberries include slugs, snails, and spider mites. Diseases such as gray mold, powdery mildew, and verticillium wilt can also be a problem. To prevent these issues, make sure to plant disease-resistant varieties, practice good sanitation, and monitor the plants regularly for signs of pests or disease.

Sweet Potatoes

Sweet potatoes are a popular crop for raised bed gardening, as they require loose, well-draining soil and plenty of sunshine to grow well. Here are some plant profile details for sweet potatoes:

Soil requirements: Sweet potatoes thrive in loose, well-draining soil with a pH between 5.0 and 6.5. Raised beds filled with a mix of sandy loam and organic matter can provide the ideal growing conditions.

Sun exposure: Sweet potatoes need full sun to produce a good crop. Make sure your raised bed is located in a spot that receives at least 6 hours of direct sunlight per day.

Watering: Sweet potatoes require regular watering throughout the growing season, especially during dry spells. Aim to keep the soil evenly moist but not waterlogged.

Planting: Sweet potato slips (small plant starts) should be planted in warm soil after the last frost date in your area. Space slips 12-18 inches apart in rows that are 3-4 feet apart.

Fertilization: Sweet potatoes benefit from regular fertilization with a balanced fertilizer (e.g., 10-10-10) throughout the growing season.

Harvesting: Sweet potatoes are typically ready to harvest 100-120 days after planting. Wait until the leaves begin to yellow and die back before harvesting. Carefully dig up the tubers using a garden fork or shovel, being careful not to damage the roots. Cure the harvested sweet potatoes in a warm, humid place for 10-14 days before storing in a cool, dry location.

Tea Plant

The tea plant (Camellia sinensis) is an evergreen shrub or small tree that is native to Asia. It is grown commercially for its leaves, which are used to make tea. Tea plants can also be grown in raised beds for personal use.

Here are some plant profile details for tea plants:

Growing requirements: Tea plants prefer acidic soil with a pH between 4.5 and 6.0. They require well-draining soil that is rich in organic matter. Tea plants grow best in full sun to partial shade.

Planting: Tea plants can be grown from seeds or cuttings. If growing from seeds, they should be soaked in water for 24 hours before planting. Cuttings should be taken from mature plants and rooted in a potting mix before transplanting to the raised bed. Tea plants should be spaced at least 4-6 feet apart.

Care: Tea plants require regular watering, especially during the growing season. They should be fertilized every two weeks with a balanced fertilizer. Prune tea plants in early spring to promote new growth.

Harvesting: Tea leaves can be harvested when they are young and tender. The top two leaves and bud are usually picked. Harvesting should be done in the morning when the leaves are dry. Leaves can be dried and processed to make tea.

Pests and diseases: Tea plants are susceptible to pests such as aphids and spider mites. They can also be affected by diseases such as root rot and blight. Proper care, including regular pruning and fertilization, can help prevent these problems.

Tomatoes

Tomatoes are one of the most popular plants to grow in a raised bed garden, and for good reason. They're easy to grow, produce high yields, and are incredibly versatile in the kitchen. Here are some key things to know about growing tomatoes in your raised bed garden:

Variety: There are many varieties of tomatoes to choose from, each with their own unique flavor and growth habits. Consider factors such as size, shape, color, and taste when selecting a tomato variety for your garden.

Soil: Tomatoes prefer a well-draining soil with a pH between 6.0 and 7.0. Amend your soil with compost and other organic matter to improve its structure and fertility.

Sunlight: Tomatoes need at least six hours of direct sunlight per day to thrive. Choose a location for your raised bed garden that gets plenty of sun, and consider using a trellis or other support to maximize your plants' exposure to light.

Watering: Tomatoes need consistent watering to prevent blossom end rot and other problems. Water deeply once or twice a week, rather than shallowly more often, to encourage deep root growth.

Fertilizer: Tomatoes are heavy feeders and benefit from regular fertilization. Use a balanced fertilizer or compost tea every two to three weeks throughout the growing season to support healthy growth and fruit production.

Pruning: Tomato plants benefit from regular pruning to promote good air circulation and prevent disease. Pinch off suckers that grow between the stem and branches, and remove any yellowing or diseased leaves.

Harvesting: Tomatoes are ready to harvest when they've reached their full size and have a rich color. Pick them as soon as they're ripe to prevent cracking or splitting, and store them in a cool, dry place.

Turnips

Turnips are a cool-season root vegetable that can be grown in raised beds. Here are some plant profile details for turnips:

Soil requirements: Turnips grow best in well-drained soil with a pH between 6.0 and 7.0. The soil should be loose and friable to allow for good root development.

Sun requirements: Turnips require at least six hours of full sun per day. They can also tolerate some shade.

Water requirements: Turnips require regular watering, especially during dry periods. The soil should be kept moist but not waterlogged.

Planting time: Turnips are a cool-season crop and should be planted in early spring or late summer. They can also be planted in the fall in mild-winter areas.

Spacing: Turnips should be planted 4 to 6 inches apart in rows that are 12 to 18 inches apart.

Fertilizer: Turnips do not require a lot of fertilizer, but they will benefit from a balanced fertilizer applied before planting.

Pests and diseases: Turnips can be susceptible to flea beetles, root maggots, and clubroot. Practice good garden hygiene and crop rotation to help prevent these pests and diseases.

Harvesting: Turnips are ready to harvest when the roots are about 2 to 3 inches in diameter. The greens can also be harvested and eaten as a nutritious vegetable.

Storage: Turnips can be stored in a cool, dry place for several weeks. The greens should be removed before storage.

Watermelon

Watermelon is a popular fruit that can be grown in raised beds. Here are some plant profiles for watermelon in raised bed gardening:

Planting time: Watermelon seeds should be planted in late spring, after the last frost has passed and the soil temperature is at least 60°F (15°C). The ideal soil temperature for watermelon seed germination is between 70-85°F (21-29°C).

Sunlight requirements: Watermelon plants require full sun exposure, which means they need at least 6-8 hours of direct sunlight per day. Make sure to choose a spot in your raised bed that receives plenty of sunlight.

Soil requirements: Watermelon plants prefer well-draining soil that is rich in organic matter. Before planting, amend your soil with compost or aged manure to provide the nutrients that watermelon plants need to grow.

Spacing: Watermelon plants need plenty of space to grow and spread out, so make sure to plant them at least 3-4 feet (0.9-1.2 meters) apart in your raised bed.

Watering: Watermelon plants require regular watering to ensure that the soil stays moist but not waterlogged. Water deeply once or twice a week, depending on the weather and soil conditions.

Fertilization: Watermelon plants benefit from regular fertilization with a balanced fertilizer that is high in nitrogen. Apply fertilizer once a month throughout the growing season.

Harvesting: Watermelons are ready to harvest when the fruit is fully ripened and the underside turns yellow or cream-colored. To check for ripeness, thump the watermelon with your finger – a ripe watermelon will produce a deep, hollow sound. Cut the watermelon from the vine with a sharp knife, leaving a few inches of stem attached.

Zucchini

Zucchini is a warm-season, summer squash that can thrive in a raised bed garden. Here are some plant profile details for zucchini in a raised bed garden:

Soil requirements: Zucchini prefers well-drained soil that is rich in organic matter. It's important to ensure that the soil in your raised bed is fertile and has a pH level between 6.0 and 7.0.

Sun requirements: Zucchini needs at least 6-8 hours of direct sunlight per day to grow and produce fruit. Make sure your raised bed garden is located in a spot that receives ample sunlight.

Watering requirements: Zucchini needs consistent moisture to grow properly. It's important to water your zucchini regularly, ensuring that the soil is evenly moist but not waterlogged.

Spacing: Zucchini plants need plenty of space to grow and spread. Make sure to space your plants at least 3 feet apart in all directions to give them room to grow.

Fertilization: Zucchini is a heavy feeder and requires regular fertilization to produce abundant fruit. You can use a balanced, organic fertilizer or compost to provide the nutrients your plants need.

Pest and disease control: Zucchini is susceptible to a variety of pests and diseases, including squash bugs, cucumber beetles, and powdery mildew. It's important to monitor your plants regularly and take action as needed to prevent and control these issues.

Harvesting: Zucchini is ready to harvest when the fruit is about 6-8 inches long and the skin is firm and glossy. Be sure to harvest your zucchini regularly to encourage continued production.

Harvesting is the culmination of all the hard work you put into your raised bed garden. Here are some tips to help you maximize your harvest:

Know when to harvest: The timing of your harvest will depend on the type of plant you're growing. Some plants, such as herbs, can be harvested as soon as they reach maturity, while others, such as tomatoes and peppers, may need to ripen on the vine before they're ready to pick. Consult a gardening guide or the seed packet for specific instructions on when to harvest each plant.

Harvest at the right time of day: It's best to harvest your plants early in the morning or late in the afternoon, when the sun is less intense and the plants are less stressed. This will help ensure that your plants stay fresh and crisp.

Use the right tools: Depending on the type of plant you're harvesting, you may need different tools. For example, you'll need pruning shears to harvest herbs and scissors to harvest salad greens. Be sure to clean your tools thoroughly after each use to prevent the spread of disease.

Harvest gently: When harvesting your plants, be sure to handle them gently to avoid damaging the delicate leaves and stems. Use a light touch and avoid pulling or tugging on the plants.

Harvest often: For many plants, such as herbs and salad greens, it's best to harvest frequently to encourage continued growth. Be sure to pick only what you need and leave the rest to grow.

Store your harvest properly: After you've harvested your plants, it's important to store them properly to ensure their freshness and quality. Some plants, such as herbs, can be stored in a vase of water on your countertop, while others, such as tomatoes, should be stored in a cool, dark place. Consult a gardening guide or the seed packet for specific instructions on how to store each type of plant.

Enjoy your harvest: The best part of raising a garden is enjoying the fruits of your labor. Whether you're making a salad with fresh greens or cooking up a delicious dish with your homegrown vegetables, be sure to savor the flavors of your hard work.

Maintainence

Staking, trellising, and other structures can be important tools in maintaining a healthy and productive garden. Here are some common structures used in gardens:

Stakes: Staking is a common method for supporting plants that have weak stems, such as tomatoes, peppers, and eggplants. You can use bamboo or wooden stakes, or even repurpose old broom handles or metal pipes. Simply drive the stakes into the ground next to the plant and tie the stem to the stake with twine or garden tape.

Trellises: Trellising is another method for supporting plants that vine or climb, such as peas, beans, cucumbers, and squash. You can use wooden or metal trellises, or even create a trellis out of chicken wire or string. Simply train the plant to climb up the trellis as it grows.

Cages: Cage structures are another method for supporting plants such as tomatoes, peppers, and eggplants. You can use pre-made wire cages or create your own out of concrete reinforcing wire or chicken wire. Simply place the cage around the plant and tie the stems to the cage as needed.

A-frames: A-frames are a type of trellis that can be used for plants that require support, such as peas or beans. You can create an A-frame out of bamboo poles or wooden stakes, and then tie string or twine between them to create a support structure for the plants.

Hoop Houses: Hoop houses are structures made out of hoops or arches covered in plastic or fabric, which can be used to protect plants from the weather or extend the growing season. You can use

PVC pipes or metal conduit to create the hoops, and then cover them with plastic or fabric.

Maintaining a raised bed garden is an ongoing process that requires regular attention and care. Here are some techniques and tools that can be used to maintain a healthy and productive raised bed garden:
Watering: One of the most important aspects of maintaining a raised bed garden is ensuring that the plants receive adequate water. A watering can or hose with a spray nozzle can be used to provide plants with a steady, gentle stream of water. A drip irrigation system can also be installed to provide a more efficient and even distribution of water to the plants.
Weeding: Weeds can quickly overtake a raised bed garden and compete with plants for nutrients and water. A hoe or hand trowel can be used to remove weeds from the soil. Mulching with organic materials like straw, leaves, or grass clippings can also help suppress weed growth.
Pruning: Some plants, like tomatoes or peppers, may require pruning to encourage bushier growth and higher yields. Pruning shears or scissors can be used to remove unwanted or damaged growth from plants.
Fertilizing: Regular fertilization is important for maintaining healthy plant growth in a raised bed garden. A balanced fertilizer or organic options like compost or aged manure can be applied to the soil to provide essential nutrients to plants.
Pest and disease control: Pests and diseases can quickly spread in a raised bed garden and cause damage to plants. Using organic pest control methods like hand-picking or spraying with a homemade solution of soap and water can help prevent infestations. Planting disease-resistant varieties of plants can also help prevent the spread of disease.

Soil testing: It is important to regularly test the soil in a raised bed garden to ensure that it has the correct pH and nutrient levels for plant growth. A soil test kit can be purchased at a garden center or online to determine the current condition of the soil. Based on the results, amendments like lime or sulfur can be added to adjust the pH and nutrients can be added to improve soil fertility.

Harvesting: Harvesting plants at the right time is important for maintaining healthy plant growth and yields. A pair of sharp scissors or pruners can be used to carefully remove ripe fruit or vegetables from plants.

Cleaning and maintenance: Regular cleaning and maintenance of garden tools, watering cans, and other implements used in a raised bed garden can help prolong their lifespan and prevent the spread of disease. Tools should be cleaned with soap and water after each use and stored in a dry location.

Dos and Don'ts – Myth and Facts

Dos

Choose the right location: Selecting the right location is crucial for the success of a raised bed garden. Choose a spot that receives at least six hours of sunlight per day and is easily accessible for watering and maintenance. Avoid areas with poor drainage or where water tends to accumulate, as this can lead to root rot and other issues.

Use good quality soil: The soil in a raised bed garden should be of high quality and free from contaminants. Use a mixture of topsoil, compost, and other organic matter to create a rich, fertile growing medium. Good soil should be well-draining and hold moisture, while also providing adequate aeration and nutrients for plant growth.

Practice crop rotation: Crop rotation is important for preventing soil-borne diseases and pests from building up in the soil. Rotate your crops each year by planting different crops in different areas of the garden. For example, if you grew tomatoes in one bed one year, plant them in a different bed the following year.

Water regularly: Adequate water is essential for the growth and development of plants in a raised bed garden. Water your garden regularly, especially during hot and dry periods. Water deeply and infrequently to encourage deep root growth and avoid overwatering, which can lead to root rot and other issues.

Mulch: Mulching is an effective way to help retain moisture in the soil and suppress weed growth. Use organic mulch like straw, leaves, or grass clippings to cover the soil around your plants. Mulch also helps regulate soil temperature and prevent soil erosion.

Fertilize: Plants in a raised bed garden require regular fertilization to provide essential nutrients for healthy growth. Use organic fertilizers like compost or aged manure to add nutrients to the soil. Fertilize your plants according to their specific needs and avoid over-fertilizing, which can lead to nutrient imbalances and other issues.

Prune and deadhead: Regular pruning and deadheading can help promote healthy plant growth and prolong the flowering period of plants like annuals and perennials. Pruning involves removing unwanted or damaged plant material, while deadheading involves removing spent flowers.

Clean and maintain garden tools: Regularly cleaning and maintaining your garden tools is important for preventing the spread of disease and prolonging their lifespan. Clean your tools with soap and water after each use and store them in a dry location. Sharpen dull blades and replace worn or damaged tools as needed.

Don'ts

overcrowd your plants: Overcrowding plants in a raised bed garden can lead to competition for resources like nutrients and water, resulting in stunted growth and reduced yields. Make sure to space your plants according to their specific needs, and avoid planting too many plants in a small space.

Don't use synthetic pesticides and fertilizers: Synthetic pesticides and fertilizers can harm beneficial insects and pollinators and negatively impact soil health. Instead, use organic methods to control pests and add nutrients to the soil.

Don't overwater: Overwatering can lead to root rot and other issues. Make sure to water your raised bed garden deeply and infrequently, allowing the soil to dry out slightly between watering.

Don't use treated lumber: Treated lumber can leach harmful chemicals into the soil, which can be taken up by plants and harm beneficial organisms. Use untreated lumber or alternative materials like brick or stone to construct your raised bed.

Don't neglect crop rotation: Neglecting crop rotation can lead to the buildup of soil-borne diseases and pests, reducing yields and harming the health of your plants. Make sure to rotate your crops each year, planting different crops in different areas of your raised bed garden.

Don't ignore soil health: Soil health is crucial for the success of a raised bed garden. Make sure to add organic matter like compost, aged manure, or cover crops to your soil regularly to improve soil structure and fertility.

Don't ignore pests and diseases: Pests and diseases can quickly spread and harm your plants if left unchecked. Regularly inspect your plants for signs of pests or diseases and take action as soon as possible to prevent further damage.

Myth: Raised bed gardens require a lot of maintenance.

Fact: While any garden requires some level of maintenance, raised bed gardens can actually be easier to maintain than traditional gardens. The defined borders and elevated nature of raised beds make weeding, watering, and pest control easier and more efficient. Additionally, because the soil in raised beds is often a mix of high-quality compost and topsoil, it can require less fertilizer and other inputs.

Myth: Raised bed gardens are expensive to build.

Fact: While it's true that building a raised bed garden requires some initial investment, the costs can vary widely depending on the materials used. Raised beds can be constructed using a variety of materials, including wood, cinder blocks, or even repurposed materials like old pallets. Additionally, the long-term benefits of raised bed gardening, such as increased yields and healthier plants, can outweigh the initial costs.

Myth: Raised bed gardens are only for vegetables.
Fact: While raised bed gardens are popular for growing vegetables, they can be used to grow a wide range of plants, including flowers, herbs, and fruits. In fact, because raised beds offer better control over soil quality and moisture levels, they can be ideal for growing plants that are picky about their growing conditions.

Myth: Raised bed gardens are only for small spaces.
Fact: While raised bed gardens are a popular option for small yards or urban spaces, they can be scaled up to fit larger areas as well. Multiple raised beds can be connected to create a larger garden space, and larger raised beds can be constructed using longer boards or blocks.

Myth: Raised bed gardens don't drain well.
Fact: While it's true that raised beds can be prone to waterlogging if they are not properly constructed, they can actually drain better than traditional gardens. Raised beds are typically filled with a soil mix that includes a high proportion of organic matter, which can help improve drainage and prevent water from pooling in the bed.
By understanding the facts and dispelling common myths about raised bed gardens, gardeners can make informed decisions about whether this type of gardening is right for them. Overall, raised bed gardens can be a highly effective way to grow plants and vegetables, providing better control over growing conditions, higher yields, and easier maintenance.

www.ingramcontent.com/pod-product-compliance
Lightning Source LLC
Chambersburg PA
CBHW060947050726
47592CB00003B/1135